THE GREAT DIVIDE

B
E
T
W
E
E
N

I0441402

BLACKS & WHITES*

By
Jeanette Davis

*SPECIAL EDITION WITH U.S. CONSTITUTION

Copyright © 2008 Jeanette Davis

All rights reserved.

ISBN:1-4392-1825-0
ISBN-13:9781439218259

Visit www.booksurge.com to order additional copies.

This work is dedicated:

Posthumously to – Miriam Makeba

&

all people who are struggling for equality and justice throughout the world.

all people who believe in freedom, liberty and justice for all.

all of the spirits of deceased patriots who have fought for freedom, liberty, and justice for all peoples

all of the soldiers dead and alive, who fought and are fighting in wars just and unjust.

**CONGRATULATIONS PRESIDENT BARACK OBAMA
Our First Black President!!!**

"Today is ours; let's live it.
And love is strong; let's give it.
A song can help; let's sing it.
And peace is dear; let's bring it.
The past is gone; don't rue it.
Our work is here; let's do it.
The world is wrong; let's right it.
The battle is hard; let's fight it.
The road is rough; let's clear it.
The future is vast; don't fear it.
Is faith asleep? Let's wake it.
Today is ours; let's take it.

(Anonymous)

CONTENTS

Introduction

Chapter 1
Uncertain Times 1

Chapter 2
Educating Young America 35

Chapter 3
Slavery's Aftermath 53

Chapter 4
Black Men, White Women; Black Women, White Men 85

Chapter 5
A Mixed Racial Bag of Eccentricities 107

Chapter 6
Economics 161

Constitution of the United States 201

Declaration of Independence 221

Communication Can End Racism 225

Introduction

All of anything is absolute. It is not the intention of this author to categorize any person, or group, be they black or white. Everything written here is done so to stimulate thinking and debate.

Each page in this book has a lead off sentence. These sentences are phrases spoken by many people, black and white, throughout the years, and some are the authors. Some are conclusions that have been drawn. Some of the statements are untruths, and some are truthful. Some are comical, others are not. Some are ridiculous, and some are highly intuitive. All of them are vital to us understanding The Great Divide Between Blacks and Whites. This author has decided to throw in her "two cents" worth of knowledge to further drive the theme home.

Do not let the title of this book limit this discussion between Blacks and Whites. All people considered by Whites to be people of color are included in the black group due to our similarity in struggle against white supremacy. The structure of this book warrants total inclusion of Hispanics, Native Americans, Asians and immigrants from so-called "colored" countries because we all are intermixed although separated by forces that wish to remain in power through the divide and conquer concept. If ever these groups unite in the common cause of total equality in America, the political power this would create would be enough to change America's way of dealing with the racial issue.

Everyone will find some of their own conclusions, thoughts, and biases inside. This is only true because each of us own thoughts we assume others do not share. When we open up to others, we find the same thoughts, ideas, conclusions, and dialectic reasoning is prevalent and universal in scope.

Speaking truth often places one's head on the global chopping block of opinions. Writers take these chances in order to teach, inspire, inform, challenge, and to aid in the enhancement of human development and evolutionary, as well as revolutionary change. Exposing one's soul to the universe is a personal matter. Exposing one's thoughts to the world is stressful at best. The author's no-holds-barred approach may anger some, please some, and inspire others to make meaningful changes. If the latter happens, this work has fulfilled its purpose.

If Blacks and Whites truly become serious about solving the race problem in America, this book is honest enough to lay out the most profound problems that need be addressed. Someone must have the intestinal fortitude to not only reveal the awful cancer growing within America's vital organs, but to bear the stench of it while performing laborious surgery to remove it for the survival of us all.

A prime example that challenges the root of racism within Whites is the decision to vote for or against President Barack Obama. His run for office severed many people from their devotion to the Democratic Party, its values and vision for this country. This is where the rubber meets the road. To slay the dragon of racism to achieve their goals and support beliefs is the challenge they faced. Republicans who voted for him won that inner battle realizing this time that their interests were more important than their fears.

Now that a black man has attained the position of President, there is no excuse for people of color not striving to achieve their dreams in this society. The next challenge is to break down the remaining walls impeding advancement that still exist. The hope and drive in the hearts and souls of people of color have never waned, but the many obstacles they face remain as a reminder that President Obama is just one man who has through intelligence, hard work and strategy forced the door ajar. We must now realize that it is up to the rest of us to push it wide open. YES WE CAN!!!

After all is said and done, the idea of racism is totally ridiculous. People will inevitably associate and procreate with one another disregarding color, class, social, political and gender barriers as they have throughout time.

Differences are what make us exciting and appealing to one another. Mystery of the unknown motivates us to delve into each other's psyches, cultures and physical attributes. We pick from gardens of diverse vegetation because variety excites the palate. Yet, we use different yardsticks when dealing with other races as if God put a stop sign in front of us.

The reason we exist is to learn to love one another. Yet, we search the world over for answers to life's greatest mysteries, "who am I and why am I here?" Could the answer to those questions be that they are not mysteries at all? Maybe all of us are extensions of one cosmic being, but until we all realize this from the most profound level of consciousness, the fruit of life will continue to taste bitter sweet.

The U.S. Constitution has been included in the Appendix of this book. Everyone in the United States of America should have a copy in his or her library. Individuals reading it for the first time will find it very rewarding. Ignorance of the laws of the land is no excuse for violating them. This is the premier document governing the laws of the U.S. Knowledge of all it possesses is a necessity today when efforts are being made to destroy it and the protection it provides under the law. The U.S. Constitution should be read in its entirety. It is this author's intention to inform as many people as possible in order to create a more perfect Union. Enjoy!

Chapter One

Uncertain Times

Blacks have a deep-rooted scar from what has been done to them in America. The pain is so deep no amount of consolation can dull it. The hurt is so subconsciously ingrained, that even some of *them* deny its existence in order to function day to day. The denial of respectable humane existence warps the essence of the spirit. No psychologist can justify it. No surgeon can repair it. Money cannot mend it. Medication can't cure it, and words can't soothe, or heal it.

Blacks must open their Pandora's Box of pain. They must allow all the demons of past horrors to escape into the light. They must be dealt with one by one, and by their true names.

First, we'll call out loss. We call out the loss of human dignity, family, language, manhood, homeland, and self-respect. Next, we'll call on covet of riches held by others which rightfully belongs to those who slaved centuries for it. Then call on deceit, misery, death by fire, lynching, experimentation, beating, inequity in jobs, housing, etc... Call out all injustice into the light of day.

Whites *should* have a deep-seated guilt for what they know they have done to people unlike themselves in America and the world. The "Jaba the Hut" of inhumanity against others weighs heavily upon their Pandora's box of iniquities. So heavily, they refuse to open it for fear of retribution.

The problems of race will never be resolved until the deliverers of pain reveal their instruments of torture to *themselves*. No resolution can develop without honestly admitting the use of such weapons against fellow human beings.

No forgiveness can be expected until they admit guilt, and deep felt apologies are expressed. No brotherhood and sisterhood can be realized until inequities are adjusted.

Each demon within their Pandora's Box must be faced squarely. First, we'll call out white supremacy for it's the greatest evil of all. Then let oppression rear its ugly head. Greed must rise to be destroyed along with, mass murder, deceit, rape, genocide, etc...There can be no peace without justice. & THE GREAT DIVIDE CONTINUES...

(Blacks back Barack Obama?)

"He's the whitest black man they are going to find." That was an observation of a friend of mine regarding Barack Obama's candidacy for president of the United States. As painful as it may be for Blacks, this statement is true. He *is* the whitest black man. He carries himself in the way they do, has acceptable speech patterns, and relate to them as they do to each other. By pushing his white background to the forefront, he enamored himself to Whites. His white mother, grandmother and grandfather were fodder for ensuring Whites that he was not culturally black. While Blacks were attracted to his skin pigmentation, achievements and historical impact of his campaign, was this enough to ensure him of their votes? Yes.

President Obama used all of the above along with his activities in the black community to his advantage as well he should have in order to win the race. Is he as white as Whites perceive him to be? Or did he send signals culturally to Blacks that his heart is with them? That may never be known. One thing is for sure. He did not parade a white wife in front of the world. His wife Michelle fits like a glove academically, intellectually, and racially. Her image also lacks black cultural stereotypes that Whites expect from black women. President Obama's ambitions to rule the most powerful nation in the world would have been tanked had she been white or a black woman who was shown to have a little Sha Na Na in her.

Where does this leave Blacks in the equation when they are asked to support a black candidate having all of the above? What is it about President Obama that is appealing to Blacks? Did he speak to them differently than he did Whites? Did Blacks vote for him because he is black?

I venture to say that Blacks were attracted racially just as men and women are initially attracted to each other. The physical attraction is there, but after that, there has to be something of substance for the relationship to develop. The substance in President Obama is his values, plan for the nation and democratic ideals that have always been the issues for Blacks. If his administration creates the environment for all of the people to have opportunities to progress, we all win. Blacks know he is not the messiah. Father GOD reached down into Mother Africa and paired a man of her soil with a woman from Kansas to birth into being a son with the mixture of two continents to unite His children in America. Dare we waste this blessed opportunity?
Congratulations President Obama for a job well done!!!

(Whites who could not vote for Barack Obama)

No matter how white a black man or woman may seem to some Whites, they could not see themselves voting for them for President of the United States. One reason is that they have never seen a black person in that position, and cannot bring themselves to put one there. Latent or unrealized racism in some Whites emerges when time comes to pull the lever. They simply cannot accept change to that degree due to their belief that a black president would show bias towards Blacks leaving Whites outside the privileged class they have enjoyed. Their lack of understanding that this is not plausible or even possible within this society is astounding. Then there are Whites who would never under any circumstances vote for a person of color. Their racist roots are so deeply planted, they will vote against their own interests to the point of dire poverty to prevent a black person from being seated in the Oval Office.

There are also Whites who will vote against him using the excuse that he is a Democrat and they are Republicans as if no one has ever voted across party lines. Colin Powell sure changed that point of view. Turmoil visited upon all the people of the U.S. under the guidance of George Bush and his cronies to the point of economic ruin and major losses have not been enough to change those republican's perspective on their party of choice or their votes. They will go down with the ship. They are just glad their captain is white.

Religious reasons keep other Whites *and* Blacks from casting their vote for President Obama. Their beliefs are understandable and will get no rebuke from me. I'm sure in some instances race has something to do with it, but I cannot knock what is not evident.

The one saving grace in all of this is that there are millions of Whites looking out for their own interests and the best interests of the country who voted for President Barack Obama. Their support in changing the "business as usual" attitude of greed and raping of the country's coffers is to be commended. Blacks and Whites together can finally find a common goal to achieve what has been needed for a long time, decency. If we can achieve that in government, we all win.

(Blacks who didn't vote for
John McCain & Sarah Palin)

John McCain's stance on the Iraq war, his unmovable stance on a woman's right to choose, support of deregulation of the banking system, tax breaks for the wealthy, exclusion of Blacks from the Republican Party, and so many more republican views were the reasons many Blacks voted Democratic in 2008. His age was a factor to some degree, but when he chose Governor Palin as a running mate, his player card was cancelled.

Palin proved to be unread in all areas of government. She was a small time Governor with a limited view. Oops! She does have a view of Putin flying over Alaska's airspace doesn't she? But, instead of "dazzling with brilliance", she "baffled with bull—." She couldn't answer the simplest of questions put to her by Katie Couric that the average college bred person could respond to comfortably, and if not, simply say, "I don't know." She was a very poor choice for McCain's running mate. His judgment was proven frayed by choosing her. Just the thought of her becoming president if he were to become ill or die is enough to cause the whole nation to cringe with fear and indignation. She has improved by coaching, but not enough for most of us.

Blacks weren't the only ones interested in not voting for McCain. Across the board, people of all races and interests were decidedly rejecting not only McCain and Palin, but also the Republican Party and its deceptions and hypocrisies. "I am a Democrat because I have to be," is my mantra.

The Big Sell out, oops, I mean Bail out of Wall Street was the last straw. The Bush administration's decision to cover the losses of big money interests on Wall Street proved to the American people that leadership was not one of its strong points.

The decision to not consider the views of citizens caused a pause that echoed loudly throughout the nation. Phones began to ring off the hook in the House and in the Senate. Changes were made to include pork and the bill passed. Till this day many Blacks and others believe the bail out was a bad idea. Time will tell. Rebuilding is now necessary, but only with the right person at the helm. We all made a choice. GOD help us all.

(Whites voted for McCain & Palin)

Some Whites believe that only a white man can lead this country. "That's the way it's always been, and that's the way it should be." That's an opinion that needed revision and a vision. A homogeneous society needs to be reflected as such.

There are many reasons why Whites voted for McCain and Palin. Some did so because of party loyalty. Some of them had decided not to vote for McCain because of Palin's ignorance of issues. Her performance during the vice presidential debate won them over. Others did so because they wanted to avoid a tax increase for those making a quarter of a million dollars or more that Senator Barack Obama promised would occur if he were elected. No more would be the adage, "I'm a Republican because I can afford to be." Are there closet democrats voting republican just to protect their monetary interests? Sure there are, but they would never admit it.

Some Whites voted for McCain and Palin because a woman was on the ticket and they wanted to see a white woman in office before or instead of a black man or black woman. There's something about black people doing something before white people that gets White's angst up. Even when driving they can't stand to lose a standoff. They have to be first. It is something in them that compels them to the superior position and if it is not achieved, they become incensed. Not all Whites display this attitude, but enough of them for Blacks to come to a consensus that the behavior is rampant throughout the nation.

Many voted for McCain because of political advantages of power or influence in the marketplace. After money has been obtained, the next level is power, then influence. Power and influence are not bad, but rather the use of them to achieve evil objectives. The Republican Party's behavior in the past eight years is proof that its objectives were not beneficial to us all. Have the tables turned and the little guy now gets a chance to pursue happiness without relying on a "trickle-down" economy? Let's hope so. Remember that we still have a national debt to pay and a war going on in Iraq and Afghanistan.

(Blacks & Iraq)

America is a homogeneous society. This attests for the consensus of most people beyond racial lines in regard to the Iraq war. Some Blacks are in agreement that troops should be in Iraq. They believe that the country should have been invaded by our forces. I would venture to say that the number supporting this view, are few. People get caught up in fear and hype and believe whatever Washington spews forth.

The majority of Blacks see no profit in war. Black youth are sought after in schools, on street corners, in malls, and every arena they can be found for recruitment into the military by lying, overbearing recruiters. They are promised large sums in bonuses that are never received, positions in locations far away from war zones and buddy assignments. By the time they realize they have been lied to, it's too late.

The lives lost, economic drain on the economy, loss of America's moral standing in the world and personal shame for our country is overwhelmingly stressful for Blacks. To ask a people to sacrifice their children for a lie, then return to a nation that repays them with second class citizenship sends a message to the world that they are simply pawns utilized within world theater productions that are unending.

George W. Bush was deceptive from his first election vote scandal till his last day in office. The hard won rights of Blacks to vote were trampled in Florida and Ohio in 2000 and 2004. This has done nothing to win their confidence and support.

They have been bamboozled out of their homes by unscrupulous subprime lenders seeking the fast buck, lost volumes of jobs during the Wall Street debacle and suffered blaming of the victim for both. We won't even get into the effects of Katrina and their treatment by their own government. That was a travesty above and beyond the veil.

Whenever the rest of America has the sniffles; Blacks are in the throes of pneumonia. No inoculation has been forthcoming and no cure is in sight.

(Whites & Iraq)

Many Whites were also caught up in the rallying cry for war. Bush scared them so thoroughly that they were answering the call by enlisting and reenlisting in record numbers.

After the dust settled and the truth was revealed that there was no justification for invading Iraq, a sense of dread set in. They thought the invasion would be quick and precise. Instead it has been painstakingly long and handled haphazardly. They watched while the bodies of their children were shipped home in wooden boxes. They wanted to feel proud of their family members sacrificing their lives for their country to protect freedom only to feel dismayed and disappointed that their loved ones had died for a lie and the financial gain of others.

Other Whites protested the war knowing most of the perpetrators of 9/11 were from Saudi Arabia and mastermind Osama Bin Laden was in Pakistan or Afghanistan. Due to past foibles, there was no trust in Bush and his information gathering. They too would suffer the loss of loved ones, economic trials and the shame of voting a person into office responsible for the creation of their woes. Lie after lie began unraveling before their eyes. Discerning Whites not caught up in the hype protested and struggled for the most part to end the war. They saw through the lies and veil of deception. They knew there was something amiss.

Finally most Whites have awakened to reality. There are fewer of them voting against their own interests. They didn't allow themselves to be distracted by politicians as they were in the past two elections. The use of their religious beliefs and emotions to influence how they vote was easier in 2000 and 2004 when they were still experiencing the residual effects of the Clinton administration's booming economy. Bush's reign had emptied their pockets to the extent that they began to pay closer attention to the real state of the country's financial affairs. It's amazing how a squeeze on one's bank account can change one's whole perspective and political view. Now to add salt to the wound along came the Wall Street Bail Out.

(Blacks, pro and con - The Wall Street Bail Out)

Create a problem to frighten people's main sources of economic survival and a reaction is guaranteed. While scaring them sufficiently, have a reasonable solution on hand to solve the problem and they will more than likely submit to the proposal. That we can now conclude is what happened in September 2008. Bush got us again.

Many Blacks panicked and were in lockstep with the raping of taxpayer's coffers by financial corporations. After eight years of deception, they also had not learned from Bushes' past debacles. They fell for the hype and fear tactic again.

Other Blacks doubted the Bush Administration's alarm and were willing to take the chance of waiting until a new administration took office to fix the problem. Could this be a last ditch effort to empty the coffers before the first black president took office? With little to no revenues to work with, how could he possibly deliver promises made during his campaign? Was this planned by the republicans with the knowledge that there was no way for them to win the 2008 election? It makes you want to say hmmmm....

Without the bail out, it meant there would be hard times for all Americans which would have been acceptable to those particular Blacks. America had gone through hard times before. Why place such large sums of money into the hands of the same people who created the financial crisis in the first place? In the end, taxpayers would reap the whirlwind of a higher national debt with no end in sight, continued dipping into their pockets at will by failed corporations and other greedy entities for many generations to come.

The trend had been set. Lame duck President George W. Bush signed the Wall Street Bail Out bill into law on October 3, 2008 with an $110,000,000,000 pork add-on creating a sum of $810,000,000,000 or more. Bush's goal had been achieved and panic-stricken citizens, black and white, fell for it. The nation and the world may have laughed at Bush's gaffs and idiocy, but who has the last laugh now that Atlas has Shrugged?

(Whites, pro and con - The Wall Street Bail Out)

Who had more to lose on a collective level more than Whites who had invested their whole lives in the stock market in some form of investment or another? Their collective net worth in retirement, stocks and bonds, 401ks, and other investments far outweighed those of Blacks. Fat portfolios were quickly disappearing during the meltdown generated by the robber barons who found a new way to rob the coffers. Many Whites panicked also and immediately supported the passing of the legislation to stop the economic bleeding.

Others were reluctant and said, "Hold on there, buddy, why the rush?" They could see beyond the immediate danger. Their approach to the so-called meltdown was to let the market correct itself and in time everything would settle down without taxpayer's money being used to intercede. The market did just that two days before the Bail Out bill was signed. But it was too late. The stampede was out of control. The Senate and House had bargained and appeased lobbyists behind closed doors to obtain votes for passage of the bill and in the process the 700 billion dollar proposal had ballooned into 810 billion plus. The die was cast. Over 400 of the country's most brilliant economic minds had been ignored along with angry taxpayer's calls to legislators to kill the bill. The bill was passed and new economic woes are now upon us. The full extent and length of time economic downtrends will continue is unknown. It is the unknown that frightens many Whites and all citizens looking for answers from those in charge of their economy and futures.

The country came to a standstill while Whites and everyone else observed how the governmental process worked without acknowledging their input. This struck home for many Whites. They began to see how out of control the government had become. Even the candidates for president ignored the will of the people.

What could McCain, a Bushite do? How could Obama *change* things? Even they had ignored the people's will. What and who could the people believe in now? What could they have faith in anymore?

(Blacks & Faith)

Blacks have survived through faith in GOD and themselves. The world recently got caught up with the revealing of "The Secret" book and DVD as if it was something new. People began to apply the principles therein to their lives hoping for miraculous happenings to occur. The process of "The Secret" is for one to visualize what one wants in life, ask the universe for it and believe that it will manifest.

Blacks had their own tried and proven test of faith. From the bowels of slavery to present day, they have looked to Jesus and Father GOD for their needs and desires. They have asked, visualized, believed and received untold blessings. They have been through the Valley of the Shadow of Death, survived the fires of Hell (slavery) dodged the slings and arrows of injustice and continue to this day to struggle against targeted destruction and degradation.

A white Christian bookstore clerk once said to this author, "Black people are more spiritual, you know." I replied, "We've had no choice. We had to believe in GOD. There was no other option." I went on to explain to her that in Africa belief in the Creator was a way of life, not a weekend pastime and had not lost its impact on Blacks genetically.

There may be a few Blacks wandering in delusion of whether there is a GOD or not, but most of them know that GOD exists. How do they know? They can feel Him. Melanin has more power than any scientist can begin to imagine. No test can gauge its true essence. Its' properties create a connection to GOD that can only be experienced by those in possession of it.

Many used "The Secret" throughout time to destroy Blacks, but GOD had His own agenda and Blacks are still here thanking Him daily.

So does this mean that Blacks have faith that everything will be all right in the long run and America will rebound after this economic downturn? This cannot be collectively determined, but they do know that with faith anything is possible. With faith, *everything* is possible. One thing is for sure. Suicide is not an option.

(Whites & Faith)

There are many good white Christians who truly worship GOD, have faith, and live by faith daily. They too have had their experiences where GOD has shown Himself to be real in their hearts and lives. They attend church regularly, tithe and consider themselves devout Christians. They live the lives they sing about in their spiritual songs. Yet, some cannot rise above racist teachings of the past. They just can't bring themselves to stomach people unlike themselves. Those old tapes keep rearing up separating them from the love of their fellow Christians who are gay, minorities and exercise the free will GOD gave us all to make choices.

Then there are Whites who see money as their GOD. They have faith in money, honey. That is not to say that some Blacks don't have the same warped values. Greed is their driving force. Usury, scams and legal robbery sustains their faith in themselves only. They see GOD as an illusionary figure that is created to be an opiate for the masses.

The Wall Street carpetbaggers are a prime example of greed at its highest degree. They flaunt this behavior in the face of GOD thinking there will not be repercussions. They are not historically astute.

All faithful church going white people are not holy. Ma Barker of the Barker Gang was an example of that. She was a church going woman who purposely raised her sons to become ruthless criminals. In the end, she went down in a blaze of glory in a shoot out with the police. Where is that set of values in the Bible? *Mr. World went to church never missed a Sunday. Mr. World went to Hell for what he did on Monday.*

Then there are the true Christians. They live according to the Word of GOD in every aspect of their lives. These are people who not only go to church, but also seek ways outside of the church to carry on the teachings and the word of GOD. They see all people as equals and children of GOD. They are the saving grace from all of the above. They have and are destroying their demons life placed upon them to get to the throne of GOD. They know that inequality exists and fight for the rights of all people.

(Blacks killed in communities across America are mourned by their communities and are presumed by Whites to be victims of drugs and crime)

Every time a black youth is killed, the above assumption by white media, Whites and many Blacks are readily drawn. Violent death has become a common way of life in some communities. Black on black crime is easily explainable. But no matter the reason, black people have great love for their children, husbands, wives, daughters, brothers, sisters, and extended family members no less than any other community of people. The sting of death is tragic and its cause does not lessen it.

Black on black crime stems from self-hatred. Feeling trapped in undesirable situations and circumstances with others like oneself can eventually lead to feelings of familiarity, which we know, leads to contempt. Slavery's impact is engrained. Feelings of alienation and hostility by and from Whites, when venturing out of familiar surroundings, pushes one back into a dichotomy. It is ones' comfort as well as ones' danger zone. Feeling *locked in* is not an individual observation. It is communal.

Communities with large numbers of people perceiving themselves trapped, or locked in, have a very high degree of rage. This rage seeks an outlet, and more often than not, an innocent person becomes its victim. The person committing the crime is not always a drug dealer or criminal. Neither is the victim always participating in criminal activities. Both *are* victims, but strictly from a circumstantial point of view.

People involved in criminal activity are predators seeking innocent victims. These people create situations that may end in maiming, crippling or death. They prey on their own.

Regardless of how death occurs in black communities, the loss is deeply felt. Lives of the living are changed forever. The community is haunted by specters of the dead pleading for someone to do something to affect change. Black communities across America have bled enough. The death watch continues and blood continues to flow. Who will stem it?

(Whites killed in communities across America are eulogized as innocents slaughtered and cut off in their prime of life. Their lives are presumed more valuable and precious than black lives)

Without awareness of it, news media makes a big deal of violent deaths in white communities. The search for answers, suspects, neighbor's comments, family interviews, funeral footage, and follow up may go on for weeks, months and sometimes years. The assumption that the media is not aware of the extra emphasis they put on white tragedies is because most media persons are white and see themselves as valuable persons.

To be fair, unintentional racism is most often the cause for a lot of preferential things Whites do for themselves and their own than conscious vindictiveness toward others.

They portray white victims as angelic personages with great potential before death. No matter how terrible a person may have been, they are given the benefit of positive reflections. Criminals are excused as psychologically deprived regardless of the crime.

The media has dissected every white serial killer's life. There is a hunger within Whites that has to be fed and the media knows it. Whites want to be assured that their family members will not succumb to such behavior. They want answers. What happened in the criminals' lives that caused them to *snap*? Where did their parents go wrong? Could this happen to them or their relatives and friends? What are the warning signs? The media have many programs to answer those questions. *Snapped, City Confidential, Notorious* and *Cold Files* are just a few of them.

Regardless of the reasons Whites commit crimes the media asserts that there must be something wrong with them. When it is revealed that white teenagers and young adults, who have had the best of everything, commit crimes for kicks, Whites are still convinced that there is something wrong with them. The young people in white communities have always been allowed to get away with wrong doing so breaking laws is just an extension of their home life. Why aren't they judged by the same yardstick as Blacks? The answer is simple. They are the privileged class. They know it and use it to their fullest advantage.

(Blacks are arrested three times more than Whites for the same crimes)

2007: Houston, Texas Police Department: The city did an audit and found that 67 percent of tasers were deployed on Blacks while they comprise 25 percent of the city's population. This practice is rampant in Houston and in many cities throughout the country. A six-year-old boy, 11 year-old mentally retarded girl, and even an 82-year-old woman were tasered by police in different cities. All of them were black. What threat could any of the above have presented to any trained police officer?

2008: Philadelphia: According to the Uhuru Solidarity Movement, Blacks have the highest poverty and imprisonment rates, 50 percent of black men are unemployed, 25 percent live below the poverty level, and there is a 45 percent school drop out rate. These statistics create the perfect storm for the increase of crime.

2008: Philadelphia Police Department: In 2008, police were captured on videotape by a Fox TV helicopter news crew pulling three black men out of a car and viciously attacking them. Many such attacks occur daily outside the range of cameras in this country. Officers have been transferred to uproot possible entrenched corruption within the 39th District of the Philadelphia Police Department. The fear of widespread corruption has been the impetus for the NAACP and ACLU to file a class action suit requesting the Federal courts take over reform of the department. The Fraternal Order of Police claims the corruption is not widespread throughout the department and fought police transfers.

2008: Los Angeles Police Department: Since Mark Furhman's testimony of illegal police practices during the O.J. Simpson trial, you would think things would have changed in all these years. Wrong! They in fact have gotten worse, but just as worse is the Chicago Police Department according to MSNBC's World's Worst Person. They tased Ms. Fletcher, the 82-year-old woman mentioned earlier. Madison Hobley, also tortured by Chicago police, was later pardoned and released from jail. He was tortured by police using electrodes to his genitals to force a confession.

(Whites see crackdowns in black neighborhoods as necessary)

Many Whites believe crime is rampant in black neighborhoods and this justifies the Gestapo tactics used by police. They see officers rounding up minorities and think the police are doing a great job in the so-called war against crime. They fail to realize that these police may be the same ones profiting off the drug trade behind closed doors, but that is not an issue, for "Law and Order" is being maintained, no matter what price "those people" (Blacks) have to pay.

The shock that a Mark Furhman could exist sent chills down the spine of some white Americans. Most of them know there are Mark Furhmans out there, but as long as they are not infected by the voracious venom, they are not outraged. When the world is allowed to see it, they cringe because in-house business is aired, and the embarrassment of it all exposed them as the emperor with no clothes. America debases "Les Miserables" not shows torture of them.

No great outrage occurred regarding Furhman's possible infringement on black citizen's rights, or corrupt actions by other LAPD personnel today. This leaves white America right where it was prior to the Rodney King debacle, unconcerned, uncaring, and wanting to ignore the cancer quickly festering within its bowel. It cannot be passed, nor can it be cured without serious surgery.

Have they forgotten that problems beginning in black America (the microcosm) usually permeate society as a whole? This is happening today.

Police upended white skate boarders because they disliked the kids' attitude. Remember the white bikers in New York that were shoved down in the street by police without cause. Although the department was sued, the beat goes on. If the abuse of power within law enforcement agencies is allowed to go unchecked, sooner or later it will devour the children of the wealthiest people (most protected in society) within *white* America.

Recent studies state that Police have extraordinarily high rates of suicide within their ranks. Could this be guilt for brutalities they have committed, or just stress from the job?

(Black youth detained by police while in groups more so than white youth)

Black youth are harassed, searched illegally, and if nothing is found, could be framed and arrested on trumped up charges. Their constitutional right to assemble is flagrantly ignored by police.

Black youth have to constantly be reminded by parents to avoid the police, and if stopped, how to act to avoid confrontation or incitement of the police officer. Most black children in urban areas are not counseled to find a police officer when they are in trouble. They are told not to. Running *toward* policemen can often end in a child being slaughtered in the street by policemen who almost always use the excuse that the approaching child was a danger to *them*.

It is commonplace for black parents to advise their children to try not to gather in large groups because of the perception by police that they are looking for trouble. In America, where it is legal for anyone to go where one wants, associate with whom one chooses, and visit neighborhoods outside of one's own, Black's freedoms are limited if policemen wish to deem them so. The very act of stopping a person without cause is unconstitutional, yet, policemen do it all the time to black youth and adults.

Black youth experience these occurrences on a daily basis somewhere in America. Black and Latino children are dying by the hands of rogue cops, and good cops who fear black youth. Their bodies are riddled with bullets (many shot in the back multiple times while running for their lives), suffocated by illegal chokeholds, and sometimes beaten to death. This does not include those found hung in their jail cells after being arrested on misdemeanors while awaiting their parents to bail them out.

When riding in cars, black youth are harassed continuously in driving-while-black stoppages. Lawsuits have been filed to stop this craziness, but the courts are not willing to believe that police are guilty of using such tactics. Could the frustration of a job never completed and ongoing permeation of crime within society be the driving force for police to use brutality on those least able to defend themselves?

(White youth congregate in large numbers, but this is seen as "Boys will be boys")

Police have more tolerance and are more congenial when dealing with white youth. One reason is the retorts police often hear from them. "Do you know who my father is?" The father is usually someone with political or economic power within the community, or knows someone who has such powers. The "hands off" policy is adhered to unless a crime is being committed outright. Most times when a crime is being committed, if it is a misdemeanor, the parents are called to retrieve their youngster, not his body hanging in a jail cell. Programs are available to tuck them into if the crime is of a serious nature, such as involvement with drugs. Jail time is alien to white youth with money.

Whites are protected in their communities. They know the police are there to protect and serve them. They tell their children to seek out police when they are in trouble. Police *do not* mistakenly shoot down white children in the streets.

On a talk show some years ago, a group of police officers defended police tactics in so-called high crime areas. The only support they received was from young white youths from well-to-do communities who saw the officers as *protectors*. The youngsters did not sit in the audience. They stayed outside for fear the predominately black audience would attack them. The stereotyping of the audience was proof of how the white youth separated themselves from people they considered different, and whom they thought deserved maltreatment.

Many people in the audience had pictures of dead black youth killed by police. Others told of abusive experiences by bad cops in their communities. This did not sway the white youth. It was clear they felt their relationship with the police was amicable.

White youth have come before justice, but the results were more lenient than that shown black youth. Case in point; Amy Grossberg and Brian Peterson accused of killing their baby in Delaware was an interesting case. Amy spent 30 months in jail while Brian saw six of his eight year sentence suspended. Had they been black would the sentences have been different?

(Blacks serve longer prison sentences than do Whites for the same crimes)

Black sentences are ten percent longer than Whites for similar federal crimes. In the west, there was a 13 percent difference, ten percent in the northeast, three percent in the south and 12 percent higher in the northwest for similar crimes as well as similar criminal backgrounds. Many studies have been done and The Research Center for Crime and the Courts at Penn State is a good source for more information on this issue.

It is standard procedure to use stereotyping when sentencing Blacks, according to Jesse Jackson. He is right. Hispanics are now being sentenced as severely as Blacks. This is racist by nature and discriminatory by design. Both groups are being warehoused purposely. Why?

White America has determined that it will not pay for the damage it has done to Blacks through the centuries. The "Contract with America", and on Blacks, is America's political way of totally negating Blacks as a group. More jails are being built to accommodate those deemed undesirable within America. Longer sentences are meted out to remove Blacks from society, and catapult them into the institutional environment of the penal system. Within this system they perform work at slave wages for corporations avoiding having to pay wages and benefits to citizens on the outside.

Death Rows of America are also swelling with those of a darker hue. It can be predicted with certainty that a black on white killing will most assuredly bring the death penalty. A white on black killing almost always ends up in time being served, light sentence, parole or probation. This is a travesty. How can white America call itself humane and continue to sell an image to the world as being the worlds' defender of humanity? The world sees what is happening in America. Let there be no doubt that the only ones fooled in 2008 are the architects of imagery, weaving their tales of falsehoods for the world's mockery. We are not amused. Could our economic fall be retribution for America's sins? Sooner or later karma has to come into play in order to restore balance within the universe.

(Whites serve less prison time than do Blacks for the same crimes)

According to United States Justice Department data, more Blacks are incarcerated by ratio than any other ethnic group in America. This can be attributed to more and longer prison sentences for drug offenses (law enforcement policy changes) than an increase in crime.

Black men are the overwhelming majority of males in prison while the number of black females in the system has risen 78%. In 2008, although Blacks are 12.32 percent of the population in the U.S., they are more than 44 percent of the prison population.

The main focus of the drug war is in black and Hispanic communities where marketing is done in the streets. Although Whites often pick up their drugs in those communities, they are well on their way when policemen move in to nab the drug dealers.

Disparities also lays in the type of drugs Whites use. Their drug of choice is powdered cocaine that brings a lesser charge in fines and jail time than does the use of crack cocaine that is prominent in minority communities.

To date, one in 15 white youth, one in eight Hispanic youth and one in three young black men are either in jail, on parole or on probation within the penal system (author's study). Disparities in the criminal justice system are due to racism, the ability to mount an adequate defense (money), mandatory sentences disproportionately meted out to minorities, and law enforcement policies focusing in on types of drugs used within certain communities. The powdered and crack cocaine law has been amended, but it still has disproportionate sentences.

Police decide whom they arrest or warn, for which charge they are to be arrested, and how severely they are to be punished be it physically or otherwise. They are the actual judge and jury before the fact. Police *on the street* executions are rampant throughout the nation. They do not have to be mentioned here because of the rapidity and frequency of their occurrences.

Black officers are another story.

(Black police officers are more prone to treat all ethnic groups the same)

At least, some of them do. Evidence of this can be seen by formation of black police organizations and associations. It can also be seen in black neighborhoods where black officers support the communities under siege. Case in point: Glassboro, New Jersey April 17, 1994. 14 year-old Eltarmaine Sanders was in a dispute with a relative and was chasing after him with knife in hand. White officer, Peter Amico appeared on the scene and shot Sanders dead stating the youth was charging at him with a knife. Witnesses and relatives disputed the officer's claim. The Grand Jury and the Justice Department cleared him. This author lived there at that time and followed the story closely.

The same officer was given the Gloucester County Police Awards Committee's Combat Cross for his participation in crime eradication. Had that child been white, it would be difficult to find any police organization willing to grant honors.

Black police officers protested with the family on the day the award was given. We shutter to think how quickly a black officer would have been shipped away had *he* killed a white child *under any circumstances* and been vindicated. He would not have gotten an award.

Glassboro, New Jersey at that time was a community where young white police officers with attitudes rode through black communities in patrol cars with high-powered rifles sitting upright on the seat beside them. There can be no doubt that the objective was to instill fear by intimidation.

There are many black police organizations like Black Cops Against Police Brutality supporting black communities across the country. They deserve and should be given credit for limiting the abuse that could very well become more extensive.

However, in 2008 many black police officers have joined that "thin blue line" and support white officers no matter how they treat Blacks. These are the ones that have subscribed to the "them against us" mentality rampant within police departments nationally.

(White police officers are more prone to treat Blacks differently than other ethnic groups)

Not all white police officers are bad cops and all black officers are not good guys. The real question is this. How does a Mark Furhman type evolve? It seems clear that a racist society would manufacture them, but other factors impact on people's lives to counteract racist actions in most cases. Things like interacting with others and coming to the conclusion that race really shouldn't matter. Whatever the reason, it has been proven that white officers are more prone to arrest, beat, frame, dislike, disbelieve and incarcerate Blacks more often than they do other ethnic groups. Statistics bear this out. The numbers of arrests indicated earlier (regarding prison terms), are arrests made mostly by white officers.

Some carry out a "reign of terror" on communities where hopelessness and helplessness exist. People without money have no power to fight back against a system that feeds on their misery. Cops that take advantage of these people build reputations, and are rewarded with promotions by their superiors for "cleaning up the streets".

How they achieve this goal often goes unnoticed. Some superiors do not want to know, they just want the job done without Internal Affairs breathing down their necks. Bad officers use this loophole to run wild through communities. They plant weapons on dead black bodies, frame suspects, kill, rob decent citizens and drug dealers, sell drugs, hustle prostitutes, and anything else to make money and feel powerful.

If these same activities are taking place in white communities, it is kept very hush-hush unless the community is underprivileged. Even these communities suffer less attacks than do black and Hispanic neighborhoods. Arrests are not prevalent as in minority communities. One can assume that police are collaborating with white criminals (taking bribes, etc.) rather than arresting them.

The object of the whole game these officers play is money and power. Their badge is the power. They want the American dream and they achieve theirs by creating nightmares for people they perceive as inferior prey while stacking money in illegal activity.

(Blacks see money being made
in the privatization of prisons)

Privatization of prisons has run rampant in almost every state of the union. Money men have succeeded in convincing states to privatize prison systems. They say they can do a better job than the states can economically. They would build them, use their own personnel to run them and the states will have one less headache to deal with while spending less money to maintain them.

This is cost effective for the states, but what happens when the prison doors close and the state is no longer involved in regulating them? *Private prisons primarily exist to make a profit and not to serve the public* [and] *private prisons have financial incentives to cut corners at the expense of inmates' constitutional rights* (ACLU, 1996).

As states lose billions of dollars in tax revenues catching and locking up prisoners, politicians see privatization as less strain on the government. The downside in corporate takeover of prisons is the lowering of employees' salaries and loss of jobs in communities.

Race is another factor. *African-Americans are grist for the fast-growing prison industry's money mill. Crime pays. It certainly does pay for those who profit from the expanding correctional-industrial complex. They include private prison operators, those who build and supply prison cells, the suppliers of food and medicine - and guards, who recently have realized a new level of clout.* (ACLU Press Release, 9/30/97). The growing network of prisons built need bodies to produce commercial goods sold at a profit for corporations. Those bodies, mostly black, are provided by the justice system that supports this economic boom.

There must be supply and demand in order for any business to remain successful. Without prisoners, this new prison system will not make money for its benefactors and shareholders. We know who America's favorite prisoners are. Will longer sentences continue to be given Blacks in order for prison handlers to make money? Are Blacks headed for extensive incarcerated slavery?

(Whites see prisons as a moneymaking opportunity)

America is now a capitalistic and gradually evolving socialized nation. This means money first, and everything else is controlled by government or governmental assignees. The recent greed on Wall Street that almost caused the collapse of the U.S. economy in 2008 was an economic disaster's perfect storm. The main question that is asked in this society when it comes down to making monetary decisions is: "what's in it for us? The privatization of prisons means money for U.S. and private corporation's coffers.

Any time there is any slither of anticipation that money can be made; many Whites are at the front of the line. To them, money is power and power is their goal.

Since privatization has arrived on the scene; all state and federal agency workers are at risk of becoming the new unemployed. The only other recourse would be to work for thousands of dollars less because privateers are seeking high profit margins to increase their cut of profits that must be divided with state or federal agencies. Uncle Sam also wants his share!

The fact that poor and underprivileged people will be negatively impacted does not deter expansion. Whites know the consequences of such actions, but individually and collectively, they know there's a minute effect. They think people in jails deserve to be there. Whatever happens to them is of their own design. The bottom line is what really matters. That's why lawmakers can coldly sit in Washington and legislate over people's destinies without flinching.

Making money in America has reached a new low. It can be a deadly business at the expense of a select group of people. A favorite foreign saying is; "You can separate an American from his woman, but never get between an American and his money."

Many people are beginning to get the message. Some will still do anything for money. These hard times will test the souls of us all. This economic transition can be beneficial or detrimental. It is the way we deal with it that **determines who and what we are. Who are we? Time will tell.**

(Black jurors seize
opportunities to "hang" juries)

The above is not a true statement. Predominately black juries do not as a rule judge differently for Blacks than they do overall. In fact, they tend to abide by dictates of law more so than white juries.

Black jurors have not been a part of the jury system in America as long as Whites. They have not acquired that "eye for an eye" attitude. They tend to stick closely to what the law requires unless bullied into submission in a predominately white jury situation.

Often lawyers will try to eliminate black jurors from juries because Blacks coming from deprived circumstances are deemed too ignorant to understand people of wealth or substance. Of course, this is not true, but it is assumed nevertheless. Blacks are also assumed undesirable because they are too sensitive to the downtrodden, or may have reservations when deliberating on sending someone to death row.

Black jurors do not require special treatment by any system of government be it federal, state, or municipal. They want to be considered on the basis of citizenship as any other person called to jury duty. Lawyers have their client's best interest to consider, so they make assumptions on beliefs that are biased that in some cases may be detrimental to their client. The black juror excused from the case may have been the one to turn the jury around in its decision to convict his or her client.

Black jurors do not come into a jury situation with the same backgrounds, life experiences, economical status, or political points of view. They are as diverse as are Whites, Asians, and Hispanics. To place them all in the same category is unfair to them and to justice in America. The first O.J. Simpson trial jurors were predominately black. White jurors did not say anyone bullied them. Because the jury was predominately black, many Whites assumed minority white jurors were bullied into acquitting O.J. That reeks of racism. The press insinuated those white jurors felt threatened, and intimidated, though not verbally, by black jury members. That tactic didn't work. White jurors denied that accusation.

(Whites use juries to "Hang em' High")

The saying, "we're gonna give you a fair trial before we hang you," did not come out of the black community. It came straight out of the mouths of Whites to criminals of all types dating beyond the Dillinger and Baby Face Nelson era. The vigilante means of ridding communities of incorrigibles has existed as long as people have been on the planet. Whites are just better at it than others.

When vicious white people want people to disappear they disappear. If they want to use the courts to do it, they use them. Changes of venue may have limited that form of disposing of undesirables, but it is still in use today. Predominately white juries have sentenced Blacks to the full extent of the law. No mercy could be ascertained. In other words, "the book was thrown at them." They considered Blacks as the "throw away" society. The tide has not ebbed regarding this. White juries are still sending Blacks "up the river" in huge numbers, while white criminals are given every benefit of the doubt. O.J. is a good example of this use of the system.

White defenses are usually centered on their upbringing. What happened in their childhood to cause such a righteous, intelligent being to commit such a heinous crime? Were they sexually or mentally molested by parents, or other family members? What trauma caused them to become psychologically disjointed to commit such a crime? These are just some of the excuses allowed white criminals when sentencing is determined.

Blacks have not been defended this way until recently, but to no avail. Even though racism has been instrumental in causing psychological damage, family structures emaciated by drugs and lead paint possibly having caused mental damage during childhood in dilapidated communities, none of the above was considered during sentencing. Blacks are considered psychologically healthy in courtrooms across the nation. In an American courtroom, Blacks are considered totally responsible beings. Any other time, Blacks are deemed inferior, mentally unstable, disadvantaged and incapable of making appropriate decisions in times of peril.

(Black lawyers try to make an impact on the justice system)

There *are* many brilliant black students applying to law schools. Harvard, Yale, Princeton, Rutgers and many law schools are recruiting them. They are the brightest young minds within the black community. Many of these individuals are thought to be "programmed" or programmable to the system and would make excellent recruits. They are highly skilled, highly intelligent and well read in western legal techniques whatever their chosen field of law.

They have been groomed for participation in the highest category of legal maneuvering. They are also groomed to be of value to white interests alone. They are the most brilliant of the brilliant and considered wasted mind power if not utilized by Whites.

These brothers and sisters are not often found in courtrooms in America fighting for the rights of people who look like them unless excessive amounts of money is being paid for their services. Although they cannot be blamed for making money, it would be in their best interest and the interests of Blacks if they were to offer legal information to the black community from time to time. As we all know, ignorance of the law is no excuse. With the expertise available, there should be no reason for ignorance within minority communities.

There are many brilliant black lawyers working in the trenches every day in courtrooms in this country who have not sold their souls for thirty pieces of silver. They work tirelessly learning the ins and outs of the court systems. They have not had the good fortune to attend the best colleges and elite universities, but their zeal to strive for justice makes them no less qualified than their Ivy League colleagues.

These lawyers work in black communities making sure middle-class and poor people understand what is happening to them and why. They put that extra effort forth when pleading for the lives of those thrown away by a society that rejects them. They look out for the interests of their people while moving up the ladder of success. Black people respect them and their achievements. Johnnie Cochran was on of them.

(White lawyers concern themselves with upward mobility)

There are a great many white lawyers concerned with upward mobility by *any means necessary*. On the other hand, there are many struggling for justice for everyone they have the luxury of choosing to defend.

The letter of the law means the law will be adhered to strictly. There will be no exceptions to any part of it and any conclusion will be enforced. Many white lawyers are using the above criteria to win case after case. They only choose cases they know they can win. The objective is upward mobility, and respect within the profession. There are no *free* cases, only vital ones. The purpose is to show their expertise to those with powers to employ them at very high salaries. Their service to any community is done for purposes of show and self-aggrandizement rather than contribution.

Some of these lawyers will use any tactic to win. If they have to legally destroy lives to reach their objectives, count the lives eradicated. If they destroy businesses along the way, consider them annihilated. Everything is strictly business, not personal... They do not have time to consider ethics or morals, only *"the letter of the law."*

Although this is a merciless approach, America was built on this way of doing business. Huge corporations did not rally because nice people had a lot of money. People had to fail, or be destroyed economically in order for winners to prosper. This just means they are using all available means to achieve their goals. The American system of torts allows such tactics, and greedy men apply extreme pressure to accomplish their goals in the gathering of revenues.

Then, there is the ethical and moral group of white lawyers. They are the ones most Americans respect. They are excellent courtroom controllers. They know the law and use it to defend people who would not normally be able to afford a good defense. They must be commended for reaching great heights while doing what is right and legal in the American justice system.

We salute these men and women!

(Blacks denounce Supreme Court Justice Clarence Thomas)

He definitely is no Thurgood Marshall. He is not a great black achiever. He is not what many Blacks would call a *black role model*. He is not a leader for justice, neither is he respected by most Blacks as a supporter for black causes. So what is he?

Justice Clarence Thomas is considered by many in the black community to be a prodigal son and that's putting it nicely. Is there room for him to change? Sure there is, but right now he is doing more harm than good. Blacks strive to move forward and upward in America. His rulings on the court have pushed race relations backward. He is *the* prime example of a "programmed" lawyer used for majority purposes.

His efforts seem to be for self-aggrandizement only. He is serving his master well. He is doing all things asked of him without regard for his people. If this assessment seems harsh, it seems so only because of his history of using race victimization as a tool to advance.

Anita Hill struck a mighty blow to his comfortable status with Whites. He was a shoe-in before revelations of his alleged gross sexual behavior surfaced. He pled to the Congress saying he was caught up in a lynching by a democratic coup d'etat. He began to speak about striving to succeed as a black man. He spoke of how his grandfather taught him how not to be a victim. Yet, he used his victimization to assure his seat on the Supreme Court. He attacked Whites where he knew they were most vulnerable. He attacked their guilt-ridden consciousness. He begged them to allow him in. In other words, he would do their bidding. Proof of his allegiance was his psychological command of "their ways" and the casting off of his own. He stated in so many words that he appreciated their culture more than the one that spawned him. He expressed it in his speech before Congress and the world.

Justice Clarence Thomas showed the world an image of a black man they rarely see. One who is opportunistically advancing himself at the expense of his dignity and race. His marriage to a white woman did nothing to enhance his image around the world.

(Whites embrace Supreme Court Justice Clarence Thomas)

"Now if all Blacks were like Justice Clarence Thomas, there would be no race problems in America." "Clarence Thomas is the epitome of what being an American is." "He used his opportunities to become a part of the greatest country in the world. He is to be commended."

Most white sentiments on Clarence Thomas show their agreement with him as a man, and the path he chose as a professional. They see in him what they want to see all Blacks strive toward, total inclusion in American society *without black culture*. They want to embrace all Blacks who become like them. It is called total withdrawal from *who* Blacks are into total absorption into *who* Whites want them to be. Justice Clarence Thomas made that transition and Whites love it. He has become one of them psychologically. That is why they could forgive his deplorable disrespect of a black woman.

Had Anita Hill been white, would this have played well in Peoria, Illinois, Lubick, Texas or Washington, D.C.? Not! He would not have needed to talk about a lynching, there might have been one. The woman would have been applauded for standing up and exposing him. He would have backed out of the nomination because he knew Whites would not have forgiven him for such an offense.

His understanding of white men boded him well. He knew they had little or no respect for black women, so he played the card and won the hand. Or did he? In the process, he lost the respect of many decent knowledgeable Whites, and a majority of Blacks. I wonder what kind of position he holds at an all-white party. How is he treated? Hmm…

He has not disappointed his republican colleagues on the Court. His voting record has been adverse to that of Thurgood Marshall. In fact, he has been one of the most fervent administrators of republican positions and decisions made *by* the court. His Affirmative Action stance was instrumental in gaining white approval in his selection to the Supreme Court. He admonished Blacks to follow his example. **No thank you, Uncle Thomas!**

(Black youth are considered by police to be criminally inclined)

The majority of black youth are beautiful people. They are law abiding in spite of the pressures police use to draw them into the criminal justice system.

Earlier in this book, emphasis was placed on police harassment and arrests of black youth and black men in order to create promotional opportunities for police. Now, we will observe the psychology behind tactics used by both police and media.

Media and police are the first professions to cry paranoia when black parents complain of mistreatment of their youngsters by rogue cops. Whites believe media and police claims because they believe in the system. They believe police are there to serve them, and they are. Police **do not serve** black communities. They serve notice **on** them! This is not to say there aren't good policemen out there, but they are not the ones in control. Bad officers have the good officers on the run it seems. If not, why haven't they come forward to stand up for what is right?

Police constantly intimidate black youths. These youth are viewed as future criminals by police and treated as such. We can only critique law enforcement actions in efforts to psychologically figure out why they do what they do. When it pertains to black youth, their intentions are obvious. They intend to utilize black youth in their day to day investigative operations within black communities. This is where police, black and white, are not afraid to bully, beat, and terrorize people they dislike.

They stop youth without reason, intimidate them into cooperating in cases that put their young lives at risk, and expect them to turn in their classmates and friends even though they personally are not involved in criminal activity. These youth talk to family members. People in black communities know what is happening, but feel they don't have the power to stop it. Police officers responsible for such actions are psychopaths with badges preying on black communities. Lately, they have become more brazen, and now terrorize poor and working class Whites. They too are now fodder for money making prisons.

(White youth are considered by police to be law abiding)

In Bethlehem, Pennsylvania, two young white females were found dead. They had been shot. No one in their community could understand why someone would want to kill them. People within the community revered them highly in the press. Media personnel swarmed their school and community asking opinions and evaluations of their character. No one had anything negative to say about them.

A young white male was charged with their murders five months later. They were killed over $400 they owed the young man for crack cocaine. Youth are assumed innocent in middle-class and upper-class white communities. This conclusion is based on them having little reason to challenge a system created to supply their hopes, wishes, dreams, and aspirations.

It is difficult for their parents to comprehend why their children consciously commit horrible crimes. The parents of the two dead girls more than likely never knew their daughters were smoking crack. The young man's parents were probably stunned to learn that their son was not only a drug dealer, but also a murderer.

This society must be careful about putting people on pedestals. History has proven time and time again that such lofty expectations will oftentimes prove disappointing. White youth are no exception.

White youth fall prey to the same situations as youth in black communities. The living may be easier, and fish may not burn on the grill, but that doesn't mean they won't be exposed to the worse addictions and temptations in society. After all, they can afford to pay for them, can't they? Their parents are busy working hard to increase status and accumulate wealth so their children can have all they need and want. Meanwhile, their children are doing exactly what they want and law enforcement officers are turning their heads because of skin color. Does *Girls Gone Wild* get your attention?

(Blacks perceive black males
to be held least in esteem in America)

This assertion cannot be denied. Black males are the largest unemployed and unemployable group in America. Their repugnant, stereotypical image in all types of media has caused Whites, *and some* Blacks, much trepidation in hiring them.

Decent black men and young males are thrown into the mix of criminal types. Although newspapers print studies of inner city crimes being committed by a few career criminals, all black males are branded with the same *criminal* label. This has not happened to any other group in U.S. history except Italians who eventually were able to assimilate into the white void.

Black males are disrespected, disliked and ignored more than any other group in America. They are spoken to in firm and hostile terms by Whites in comfortable surroundings (when there are a majority of Whites around), dismissed rudely, eyed suspiciously when shopping, cued in on by security, observed at a distance, and Whites try to avoid any contact with them on a personal level (excluding white women, of course). They are frequently watched, but ignored in one-on-one encounters.

Case in point: A television show sent young black and white men out on the streets of a large city seeking change for a dollar bill. Whites gave the white youth change. Black youth were almost always passed by, or ignored by Whites. It was as if they did not exist. They must have felt like phantoms moving amid live folks seemingly unaware of their presence (the "Invisible Man" phenomenon).

Without income, respect, jobs, and inclusiveness, many black males do not venture into a self-made economic system as the few criminal types have. It is a testament to the strong family value systems of Blacks in general that have kept the majority of black men full of hope and anticipation of a brighter future. These fine men are to be commended for participation in the **Million-Man March** in Washington, D.C. These men are the "might and strength of the race."

(Whites see black males as criminal types no matter the dress or carriage)

It is ironic that Whites fear black males when it has been proven time after time that most crimes committed on people are usually by someone within their own ethnic group. Most white serial killers do not go into black neighborhoods looking for victims. It would not be a very smart thing to do, and secondly, their presence would be obvious.

Black criminal types are not stupid either. They know crimes committed against other Blacks will not draw too much attention. At least, not as much attention as it would if the victims were white. They know crimes committed against Whites means more time in prison and steeper fines. The system has already programmed the black psyche to this fact. In-jail comparisons have educated career criminals to this reality.

Well dressed black males are susceptible to ill treatment unless they act and speak a certain way to make Whites feel comfortable around them. If Whites are secure in the knowledge that the Blacks they deal with have been totally programmed to their way of thinking and doing things, they relax. If any indication should arise where their Europeanized concepts are challenged in any way, they readily distance themselves. They actually want *chocolate flavored white clones* instead of *African flavored uniqueness*.

Educated black males *know* how to speak *the language* for Whites and Black English for themselves when relaxing. A well-educated, well dressed black male with dreads upsets white corporate America. If he speaks well, they may accept him. They cannot get past his hair to relate to him totally. This brother may have the answers to corporate problems, yet he is not allowed to participate because of the appearance that Whites readily assume is militant or *too black* when he may just be a nice guy with a liberated hairstyle. Since it is not one approved by the status quo, he is categorized. He is rejected while police academies are hiring criminals to attack men that look like him.

Case in point: In 2008, 36% of Atlanta Georgia police academy graduates have criminal records such as: shoplifting, assault and battery and carrying concealed weapons.

Conclusion

A country ruled by laws designed for some of the people will falter, stumble and die.

This country has come a long way, but it has many miles to go before it can rest. Laws are on the books to protect the constitutional rights of all citizens except for present government invasion with the Patriot's Act which cancels out those rights. The majority of people in this country cannot get justice in precincts and courts across the land without having to pay a heavy price. If it is not a feasible price, they lose their most precious possession, their freedom.

Capitalism has become entwined with socialism that in turn permeates everything we do. Nothing is safe from its infectious growth. It permeates relationships, spiritual places of worship and the law.

Because of the evil capitalism leaves in its wake, we can no longer depend on quality legal service without lucrative compensation that has flawed the sanctity of law and left many of our citizens in jeopardy and underrepresented.

Young black men without the ability to pay for justice must feel its miserable sting. They are the scapegoats of a society conscious of its sins, but too mesmerized by capital to change its cruel ways. The pitiful souls of beautiful young men and women are being sacrificed for the sins of a nation wallowing in its own degradation.

Fine raiment cannot decorate the soul. Huge bank accounts cannot buy a conscience, nor soothe it when afire. Conscious effort to embrace, free, and uplift the least among us frees the soul of its iniquity.

Fair and decent treatment of all a country's people, even within a capitalistic environment, can and will awaken within them the will to contribute, produce and abide by the laws of the land. Only all of us can make this happen, America!

Chapter Two

Educating Young America

(Black students think white inner city School Teachers are unfair)

Black students in inner-city school systems are negated by many school boards and administrators, as *uneducable*. This is gleaned from their refusal to adequately supply children with books, supplies, safe environments, and teachers trained in dealing with diverse cultures.

Teachers traveling into this type of school system are oftentimes ill equipped to deal with inner-city mentalities. They cannot deal with youngsters who are without the bare necessities in life such as proper meals, and clothing. They are not ready for children with short attention spans due to the lack of structured environments at home, and possible health problems such as lead poisoning. They are not ready for children walking through war zones on their way to school, and they certainly are not ready for the behavior problems that arise during the school day.

Black children sense the uncertainty of their teachers. They know how to manipulate them. These same children perceive the teacher as someone coming from somewhere else to tell them what to do. They do not see the teacher as a part of their everyday reality. They continue to live a life that the teacher can't begin to comprehend.

Black children within an interracial classroom setting experience isolation. White students are addressed, called on, stroked, and encouraged more often. Blacks are told to behave, nothing of significance is expected of them, and they do not fail to meet those expectations. They misbehave because they want to be considered full participants. They desperately want to be included.

White teachers *can* teach black students. This has been proven by many good white teachers who have taken the time to understand what they are dealing with in terms of *where the student is coming from* both environmentally, and culturally.

Until black children truly feel a part of a system that presently ignores them, there will be little incentive for them to excel. Many have excelled in spite of all of the above. Only time will tell how damaged they are psychologically.

(White teachers think they're "Saviors" of black children)

Some white teachers feel the black community should be thankful to them for coming to their rescue when so many teachers will move, and become registered in another state to avoid teaching in inner city schools...

Some of them have a need to feel wanted and beholding to. When Blacks see them as just people doing their job, they become defensive and treat black children with disdain. "*I really don't have to be here,*" but if I or someone *like me doesn't teach here, these kids won't have a chance in the real world.*" The kids live *in* the *real world.* Reality doesn't get any more real than facing possible death every day one comes to school.

The *missionary* attitude is what is degrading. Black communities do not want teachers to come in to save them. They want teachers, if they must be imported, to come in to teach without regard to hidden agendas. A poor child can learn. A poor child can comprehend. Marva Collins showed the world what poor children could do with proper guidance and love from the teacher. Black teachers are putting her philosophy into action and getting astounding results.

Indirect self-fulfilling prophecy can cripple a child if it is negative, and give a child a boost up if it is positive. This is what all children need from teachers. The *"I know you can do this"* attitude, and phrases like; "*Well, weren't you ingenuous to come up with that." "You are terrific." "I knew you could do it,*" and many other supportive statements encourage children to try even harder to please the adults instructing them. They try harder because they know they will be compensated for their work. Aren't we all the same in that regard?

White teachers can become a part of one of the greatest transitions in America by giving black children tools to propel them into the productive arena whole scale in spite of environmental factors impacting on them. They must let go of the *slave-master* mentality. These kids do not relate to it. They relate to love, caring and respect just like everyone else.

(Black youth feel white teachers fail to recognize their talents and skills)

Many Blacks can recall having white teachers who told them to forget about becoming anything, or anyone important. They were often told to be satisfied with their plight in service industries, and **leave** the achieving to others, meaning Whites.

Some Whites would say, "We were just trying to save you the pain and hardship of dealing with a racist society." This is odd coming from the same people who claim they are not racist. Why do they fear black achievement? Wasn't just about everything owned and operated by Whites in the early 1900s through about 1955? Why fear those who have nothing?

The answer is: **Those who have nothing, but possess drive, ambition, and hunger to prove something, will achieve.** People with these motivators pushing them forward are bound for success regardless of drawbacks, because they have nothing to lose and everything to gain. Their moral character will determine whether they enjoy what they have accomplished. So, black advancement means competition for jobs.

Black students aren't tracked into *professions*. They are tracked into lower service industry jobs or civil-service jobs (what one might call civil-servitude). The government's record is quite poor in hiring and quite active in firing minorities.

When time comes for businesses to satisfy their Affirmative Actions goals, they claim no Blacks with expertise are available. Black youth can see this game being played with their parents.

Black parents have to remind their young men and women to ignore white teacher's negative guidance, and go for their dreams. They are told to create their own agendas for themselves dismissing input from forces destructive to their advancement. Blacks have lost many doctors, lawyers, and the like because of the negative impact white teachers have had on their young peoples' dreams.

(White teachers support white male youth)

White teachers do support white males more so than any other group. They push them to excel in the presence of other children (white females and minorities) probably not realizing the others is being affected by it, or simply not caring. Studies indicate white teachers may not even be aware that they are doing it. They have been acclimated to white males being the leaders, and movers and shakers in society for so long, that they may unconsciously accept their superiority, and encourage them to excel.

White male teachers definitely have a stake in the above behavior. They are fortifying their group by sending forward and upward replacements to the front lines. And speaking of front lines, white males are the largest number of men having sought deferment from military duty during times of war by attending school, claiming conscientious objector status, obtaining letters from a parent's connection, or simply lying. They felt they were special (as their teachers and society reinforced), so whatever it took to keep them from going to war was used.

This doesn't mean there weren't those who chose to go to war. They were the poor, or middle class patriotic and gung-ho types who answered the call when their country needed them. They felt they were the only ones who could lead, order and carry out the business of war. Of course, many of them died alongside minorities.

Teacher's words of encouragement can be dangerous. They are usually the closest adult figures dealing with children on a daily basis besides their parents. Do we know them well enough to entrust our children's lives to them?

White males have the highest suicide rates in America. Are they being inspired to achieve beyond their capabilities, or is the quest to be superior just too far out of reach to grasp, hold on to, and maintain? Lest not forget the Wall Street whiz kids who turned out not to be so smart after all. The nation relied on their expertise to find out that they were greedy inept financial managers in disguise.

(Black history should be incorporated into schoolbooks)

The history of all people participating in America should be included in schoolbooks nationwide. Every group has contributed to America in some positive way, especially Blacks.

The building of America could not begin until Blacks were transported here. The Native Americans could not do it. Whites were too weak. Not even indentured servants could bear the burden that black people bore to make America what it is today.

Credit has not been given those who contributed the most to make America happen. Apology has not been given those enslaved to create livelihoods for Whites when they arrived from Europe. Equality has not been allowed for those people earning it the most through their blood, sweat and tears.

This history is so poignant and epic. It has all the earmarks of a classic motion picture greater than "**Gone With The Wind**". It should be called; **They Built The Pyramids Too.**

This history is so filled with white hatred, murder, torture, sexual abuse, misogyny, child abuse, and human misery that it's no wonder they do not want it told in its entirety. It clearly describes who they are to such a degree that they cannot bear to see their own souls before them on screen. Knowing their love for money, one would think they would have capitalized on it by now.

Like the Germans, white Americans do not want their children to know the truth of what they are capable of. They would rather let it be hidden within the souls of black folk. We cannot wait for them to do it.

It is now time for the truth to be told. History books ought to be written by black people for libraries and schools. It is time our academicians wrote of our true pain instead of books brushing lightly over it to justify tenure within academic institutions.

(Whites want their children to learn *their* version of white history)

It is beneficial for Whites if their children are exposed to their history. It sets them aside as the heroes and controllers of peoples' destinies throughout all time. This is not true, but according to *His Story* it is.

History is controlled by he who writes it from his point of view. The truth appears when someone else challenges what is written with information and artifacts.

White children are given positive strokes daily in classrooms throughout America. Almost every book read is about them, and their exploits. Other groups are never allowed to appear mightier, smarter, or more honorable than them. No wonder they become arrogant adults. They truly believe they are *Supermen*.

Young white boys are instilled with, "*You will be one of the ones who will rule the world one day.*" They are mentally programmed to believe the world will always be the way it is now. They are told a legacy has been laid down for them to carry on. What they are really being taught is exploitation of the masses of minorities. This is never really said (as far as we know), but from what is observed from without, the conclusions are easily drawn.

If America is just a place to make money and all else is just game playing, then everyone should know that. If it aspires to be what it says it wants to become, then everyone should become aware of everyone else and their contributions. It would be the wise thing to do. One should never underestimate one's competition.

After all is said and done, it would be in the best interest of Whites to teach their children truth. It is a great disappointment for children to learn there is no Santa Claus. It is a greater disappointment for them to know their parents lied about there being one. Lies do little to increase understanding, trust, and compatibility in relationships. Parents are no less culpable for their actions than they expect their children to be.

(Black colleges and universities give Blacks a more realistic view of the world)

The most instrumental institutions created by Blacks for Blacks have been black colleges and universities. Without them, Blacks would be hard pressed to compete in today's world of high tech, and entrepreneurship.

A thorough education involves understanding the seven Liberal Arts (which were brought from Africa by the Greeks and Romans), world economy, capitalism (and other forms of government), history (all), people, rules of society, and the needs to survive and compete in today's economy.

Black colleges and universities strive harder to make up for the deficit in educational preparations made by public and private schools that often cripple black students. Black schools raise the consciousness levels of black students to new heights. Rebirth for many black students happen when they become aware of who they truly are. This creates a totally different kind of being. The shell of ignorance and inferiority is shed revealing a bright, confident, intelligent and tenacious competitor in the marketplace.

This new being knows how to play by the rules. Before the transition, the rules were used against them. Now they can play a part in changing the rules, or creating a level playing field. All of this takes place because they decided to attend a black school.

White run schools indoctrinate, while black schools educate. In white institutions, there is an agenda to transform minds to their ways of thinking. In black institutions, they want people to evaluate all things.

Black schools do not try to change people; they let the educational process transform them. That is the secret to learning. You don't put something into a person to change them. You bring it out by supplying information. One cannot expect a person to act on something they do not know. Once Blacks know, there is not stopping them.

(White colleges and universities are not set up to accommodate black student socialization needs)

White institutions expect people to orient themselves to the institutions, not the other way around. Acceptance of traditional norms is expected by administrators not taking into account the needs of other cultures, or ethnic groups.

Organizations well suited to white students, may not fulfill the needs of Blacks, Asians, Hispanics, and other ethnics. This rings true for high schools also. Beau Brummels is certainly an alien club to most people in non-white neighborhoods. When non-white students try to join, it is made clear they are not welcomed or must reform their way of thinking.

Whenever a small amount of black students find themselves on a white campus, they eventually end up forming a Black Student Union. Blacks not wanting to participate are usually well-entrenched into white communities and associate exclusively with whites. They see no need for such organizations, and feel a world apart from *those kinds of Blacks*. Their white friends say they don't consider them to be black. They take such remarks as compliments gaining them acceptance into a group they think all Blacks want to belong to. Eventually, they find themselves in situations where the color of their skin will force them into reality. What a rude awakening that is.

Black students on white campuses also find themselves in such a minority, that sooner or later, they may find themselves dating Whites. This is no abnormality today. Blacks and Whites not only date, they also marry. Where there is little availability of black males and females, they use options open to them whether they want to or not.

Sports heroes find themselves caught up in the same situations, and often end up marrying Whites. It is easy to gradually fall into the trap of assimilation. Once there, one becomes acclimated, and tend to relate to white-only activities. Therein lay the problem. They are cut off from the black community which is their nurturing base. Without it, they are absorbed into the alien environment.

(Black males need black men to guide them scholastically)

Black males educated in today's educational system and in the past are rejecting that system that has shown them rejection over a long period of time. The first contact with that society is within the school system. This is where they feel most rejected. By the time they enter into the fourth grade, they are lost and disinterested.

Programs have been designed by professional black males to teach young black boys through a process of nurturing, achievement orientation, and a positive self-fulfilling prophecy. Black boys are responding well to this new phenomenon which has been criticized by many, black *and* white.

Any experiment by blacks that will save black youth is commendable. Unless opponents are coming up with programs of their own to help these kids, they should be silent, and await the results. Criticism from the white community is expected, but within the black community we should applaud all efforts by brothers and sisters to help our youth.

Most black males in the inner-city and in some rural areas do not have positive male role models to idolize. The males they are more apt to follow are into criminal activities. They need other views of black males to give them options. They need to know that grown men were once in the same situations as themselves and were able to create better lives through educational excellence, and hard work.

Young black boys need direction and guidance that goes beyond that of black females. Black males are an endangered group. They destroy each other in acts of bravado. Such energies need to be channeled into nonviolent activities. Professional and other decent black males are the only ones capable of guiding them through the process. They have dealt with this society on their own terms and have been successful at figuring out what black males need to do psychologically in order to feel good about themselves. No matter how hard they may try, black females cannot understand the unique black male experience in America.

(White male teachers are detrimental to black male student success)

One does not tell one's enemy how to take over one's castle.

It is probably news to many in the white community that some white teachers are tracking minority students differently than white students. Then again, maybe tracking black students is old news for some people. The good news is *the black community now knows it.*

White male teachers should be seriously scrutinized. Their guidance should be investigated thoroughly before moves are made to adhere. There are some white instructors in universities who are engrossed in helping brilliant students no matter the color. These teachers are often considered *tenured renegades* who will put a wrench in the system just because they know they are not well liked and accepted into hypocritical cliques. They know the system well, and abhor it.

If black males are willing to assimilate (give up their culture); they may be allowed to participate in some activities, but never in the inner circle. They are given a peek into that which they can never really become a part of. Some black males think they have cracked through, but time will assure them of their erroneous assumptions.

White male teachers use superior-inferior attitudes with black males that are relaxed when dealing with white males. To watch them in action is an education in itself. Their mannerisms, facial expressions, and attention span are quite different with each group. Oops, there goes another trade secret!

This author has changed her son's instructor many times during his elementary and secondary school years because of the above detrimental behaviors by his white male teachers. At college level, it is up to students to take the reins when they see this occurring. It is the parent's job to alert them to what is not being said, but imparted in subtle ways. With this input, they can rise above the insult to get the education sought.

(Black females are treated differently than black males by white teachers)

Black female students are not considered a threat, so they are a little more acceptable to white teachers. Teachers see them as not having an impact on society in any great way. They will probably grow up to become single parents, end up on welfare, or work on a low wage job for the rest of their lives. They don't, as a whole, envision them going to college, or becoming anything of great significance unless their parents show interest, and can afford it.

Black girls in school today are different than those in the past. Thirty years ago, they were respectful and did minor things in class. All in all, they behaved themselves and did what was asked of them. Today, in the inner city, they bring chips on their shoulders from outside into the classroom. The teachers have to deal with spill over arguments and fights within the classroom setting. Overwhelmed white teachers are willing to deal with female disagreements more so than male.

Black males tend to intimidate white teachers. Hearing about black males killing each other causes much trepidation in white teachers who feel they may be victimized outside the of classroom if they deal harshly with them. The males know this, and rule many classrooms.

Black females often protect teachers from the wrath of fellow students. They tend to be outspoken, and will *step to* classmates who may be causing problems for the teachers. Some of them will sit quietly hoping sanity will return long enough to get in a good day's school work. If teachers are absent and a substitute comes in, everyone is prone to become rowdy. They consider it a free period to do as they choose. When this happens, the girls are often the loudest and rowdiest.

Many white teachers rely on black female and male teachers to assist them in restoring calm to classrooms. Others just give up and let students have their way. Black female gang members are joining in on the intimidation of teachers. They have given in and given up. Where they used to sidestep gang activity, they now participate to get the approval of young thugs who woo them.

(White teacher's respond to white students)

Studies show white teacher responses to white students differ in regard to sex.

White female students are expected to behave, but are handled with respect, and spoken to in a fragile manner.

White boys on the other hand are challenged constantly to excel. They are treated as if they are already professional scientists, doctors, lawyers and the like. The constant refrain heard in after class discussions is; "If you are going to be a lawyer, you are going to have to...."

They all seem to come from a happy place where misery is unavailable and unacceptable. In that happy place, perfect parents exist, all needs are satisfied, kids with credit cards and cars is the norm, and minor annoyances like acne is the biggest problem this year. No one wants to hear about real problems. Their parents take care of that kind of stuff so they can enjoy growing up.

Many white teachers feed into this mentality. They can relate to this kind of life for they are products of the same environment. Anything outside of it is disturbing to their fabricated world away from the madness of the rest of society.

When busing brought minorities into the suburbs; unheard of problems were bused in with them. Words like "wow, man," "far out," and others began to resound when word came of a black classmate having major problems in his neighborhood, or some event outside their understanding occurred. Lately things are changing.

White students are now committing horrible crimes in schools across America. Guns are being brought to school; people are being shot, beat up, bullied, raped and killed. Teachers lost in yesteryear's **Wayne's World** state of mind, are now catapulted into **Lethal Weapon III.** This does not change their way of dealing with students, however. Parents still want the illusion of *everything's okay* to continue.

(Black teachers understand black students)

Most black teachers understand black students, and try to fill voids that exist. Sometimes they can and sometimes they fail. It is difficult to understand diverse problems that may arise in a classroom setting.

The key word is "try." Black students appreciate black teachers understanding of their culture, slang, and dress. They appreciate that they do not have to explain what's going on in their lives away from school in detail (that may have an impact on their behavior) like they have to do with white teachers.

Black teachers try to break through all the environmental factors in order to reach the genius they know exist within these kids. It's one of the most difficult jobs today, but a most rewarding one when students succeed in spite of the odds, and go on to college. The same environmental factors may cause a white teacher to give up on the students. They see no hope for them. Students pick up on these vibes and draw the conclusion, "Well, if Ms. ------ thinks I can't do it, and she's the teacher, then I guess I can't." This defeatist attitude has slaughtered many a dream.

Black teachers will visit student's homes in order to work with parents instead of on their own. They know quite a few parents are barely making ends meet, working more than one job, dealing with other family problems, and just cannot adequately deal with teenager's problems during puberty. Once family problems are understood, teachers can better deal with teenagers. Some children they have helped, but others have been lost to the streets. Some black teachers have even adopted children suffering the tragic loss of parents. One fantastic example of such a teacher is Father Clemmons. There is no need to further introduce him, the black community knows him well.

Without black teachers, so many more children would be lost in an educational system that devours its young.

(White teachers do not understand black student needs)

White teachers, no matter how hard they try, do not understand the mind set of black students. They do not know how to treat them in a classroom setting. Trial and error is the norm under these conditions. If the teacher is successful in winning a student over, he or she thinks the same method will work on all black students.

Students respond most to kindness and love. If white teachers could offer those two human emotions with sincerity, kids would sense it and respond in like kind. How often does one see students in school crowding around certain teachers? One may ask, "Why do they like him/her so much?" The answer is simple. They know the person cares about them. No matter how often that particular teacher may chastise them, they never disrespect him/her.

Some black students also need time to adapt to a structured environment. Some inner-city youngsters may not come from homes where structure was an important part of their lives. All in all, most black students do come from structured environments. These students err when they emulate the most popular students who just happen to be the most unruly.

White teachers must be able to discern who the ring leaders are, find the causes of their disruptive behavior, remedy the situation, and regain control of the classroom. Sometimes this may mean removing the student, or students *from* the classroom. This may sound easy, but dealing with erratic behavior can become time consuming and exhaustive. Unless a teacher is dedicated, it may be too impossible a task to achieve. That is why many white teachers give up and quit.

White teachers need to take time with students outside of the classroom setting to get to know them as individuals. Dealing with white adults may be alien to some black students, so a little extra time spent talking to them may strip away the veil of mystery. Teachers unwilling to do this will find themselves lacking in communication skills within the classroom. Language is becoming so warbled with the impact of rap that even black and white parents have problems deciphering what is being said by today's teens.

(Black parents want excellent educational institutions in their communities)

All parents want the best for their children. Black parents are no different than anyone else, although the road to perfection is much more difficult for them.

Education has not always been available for Blacks. There was a time when it was forbidden for Whites to teach Blacks to read and write.

The mere mention of doing so would land them in serious trouble. Black slaves were not allowed to have books of any kind in their quarters. Hundreds of years of denial from what is considered the norm today among all groups of people, has left an indelible disadvantage upon the collective ability of Blacks to reach parity with Whites.

One would think the ruling, **Brown vs. the Board of Education** would have solved the problem, but there is still an overwhelming difference in the level of education provided for Blacks in respect to that provided Whites. The lack of separate, but equal education has a new excuse today.

It is fashionable for politicians to say, "The black community's tax base does not provide for schools with all the trimmings. White flight has taken part of the tax base with it to the suburbs." If this is true, it is the State's responsibility to equally divide the funds across community lines to assure all children a decent education. Trimmings can be lessened in the suburbs to provide books, supplies, and computers for schools that can't afford them in the cities. States do it all the time for other needs. Why not invest in the future of all children, not just those who can afford it?

Black parents expect the taxes they pay to reward their communities with schools that have toilets that flush, clean water, clean bathroom areas, safety, and safeguards during emergencies. They deserve better, and should vote accordingly. And we wonder why black children are not going to school? Take a good look at the buildings and the facilities within them that they use on a daily basis.

(Whites do not care about minority education)

It really doesn't matter whether Whites care about minority education or not. What does matter is whether the educational system is doing the job it was designed to do. If it is, the results could be measured statistically. If not, that too can be proven with numbers. So far, the numbers are disproportionately slanting downward in non-white communities.

It appears that students are ready for the space age while old-fashioned techniques are still stringing beads. Math and science are not two of American students' favorite subjects, be they black or white.

Computers may be the answer to this dilemma. They capture the interest of all students. Once they familiarize themselves with them, students take control of a learning tool that is not required to speak, chastise, anger, or control them. They can learn at their own pace, and monitor their own progress. This may very well be the future of education.

Race would not matter in such a scenario. The mind would find its own niche to enrich itself (with teacher supervision, of course). Students exposed to technology today will control the future tomorrow. The only concern is the biological, emotional and psychological affect it will have on them. Time to practice social skills must take precedence over technology for students to become well-rounded adults.

All children, black, white, yellow, brown, and red should have a computer. All schools should be about the business of securing them from corporations and businesses willing to donate them as tax write-offs. With computers, children can be taught all subjects visually while actively taking part in their education. Hands-on activities will leave little time to misbehave. This could be the answer to educational disparity among the races.

All of us should care about the plight of all America's youth. The only requirement is unity in requesting total government support for the advancement of all children for they are our future.

Conclusion

The educational system in America is lacking in many ways. The most common problem in minority schools is the lack of supplies. Many urban schools do not have books for students to take home to complete homework assignments, while suburban schools have books, computers, and very sophisticated equipment.

This unfair distribution of revenues to schools by Boards of Education, and State Legislatures sets the stage for minority youth to fail. The claim of tax base differentials does not sit well with black parents contributing taxes to city and state coffers. The huge flow of money into suburban areas is made possible by people in decision making positions. They more than likely are white, and live in the suburbs.

The disparity in economic support of schools in both areas does little to quell negative criticism of urban student test scores, and overall scholastic progress.

White educators prefer higher income based schools to the poor urban ones. They compete for placement, and when the short straw is drawn, they reluctantly show up for work. Many of them dislike the area, people, and poverty often associated with the district where they are assigned. When they are unhappy, their students suffer.

These teachers should be given diversity training. There *is* hope for them. Understanding is crucial. They trained for the profession to have an impact on young people's lives or so they say. This has to be true, because teachers are not paid large sums of money. There is no better place to impact children's lives than in urban schools. This is where they can test their mettle. This is where good teachers are needed most.

Chapter Three

Slavery's Aftermath

(Blacks experienced slavery in America)

There is no escaping the harsh reality of blacks having been slaves in America. There is no white escape from the harsh reality that some of them are the descendants of the men and women who enslaved Blacks, and sympathizers of the system of government that condoned it. There is no escape from the fact that today's problems in the black community are directly related to that past.

Knowing all the above to be true, Blacks and Whites are caught in a dilemma neither wants. The problems become more profound as time passes. It is time to face them, get to the root of their causes, cure the disease, and become healthy. During this process, Blacks and Whites can settle the race issue forever, but the medicine may be distasteful. It will take facing all the wrongs done to Blacks be they, physical, emotional, psychological, spiritual, or economical. The diagnosis needs to be done. It will mean working together to set guidelines to restore health in each area.

It will mean calculating what is owed Blacks economically for forced, free labor for over three hundred years. Blacks must sit at the negotiating table with the United States Government to determine what is fair and equitable to all, and the time period necessary to meet that goal.

There is no other alternative. The question of race cannot be settled until retribution is made for injustices done. Whites will never respect Blacks until they have made payment on a debt they *know* they owe. They must have known this day was coming. Did they think Blacks were going to allow them to sidestep the issue forever, or did they believe Blacks would forgive the debt? If Blacks were to forgive the debt, the world would look upon them in contempt, and say, "Those are a people with no respect for themselves. They have been used, abused, and enslaved, and still they lick their master's boots."

Blacks must demand what is owed, and not accept America's welfare programs.

(Whites feel and think they don't have to pay for slavery)

Whites living in America, whether immigrants or not, do not consider themselves responsible for what was done to Blacks during slavery.

They do not feel they should be held fiscally accountable. If this logic is correct, what about the national debt? They are not responsible for that debt either, yet, there is no doubt it will be paid, and they will pay their share of it (hopefully). It is just a matter of how and when it will be paid. Logic seems to lose its reasoning when it involves Blacks and Native Americans.

When people come to America to become American citizens they are embracing the country's responsibilities. If America has unpaid bills, they are required to help pay them. If America has enemies, they, or their children are required to fight in wars or conflicts against those enemies. If America has problems, they become their problems. They can't consider themselves Americans for some things, and disqualify themselves on others. The argument that they are not responsible for any particular situation does not excuse them from the obligation.

Another argument is, "I wasn't the one owning slaves, why should I be required to pay for someone else's crime?"

America is a Judeo-Christian country. That means it adheres to Jewish and Christian doctrines. It would seem fair to assume that most Americans are Christians. If so, the Bible states that *the sons shall pay for the sins of the fathers*. In America, the forefathers have sinned against Mother Africa's children. Our Creator saw through man's folly, and slipped a *clause* in His contract with His children.

There is no way out logically, and no way out spiritually. The only options are for White Americans to continually sin against those who have done them no wrong, or to pay what is owed. No peace will America realize. No isolation from natural disaster will be her shelter. No long-term periods of economic growth will become reality. No end to strife can take place until America does right by Mother Africa's children.

(Blacks lost family structures during slavery)

It is common practice within European societies to place minorities into situations, then years later, use it against them. This is evident in black family structures.

During slavery, the majority of black families were not allowed to create a cohesive family unit. Family members were sold to other slave owners in exchange for other slaves, money to pay off debts, acquire revenue, and numerous other reasons. The slave's value to the slave owner for economic purposes superseded family structures. Therefore, to sell a slave meant no more than selling a head of cattle. The slave's separation from family was of little concern to the slave owner, and if it was, sometimes whole families were sold and later broken up and sold off by new owners.

Today, all family structures are studied. Black families are categorized statistically to show how terribly disintegrated they are. For instance; by 1990, it was estimated that 2.69% of white women, as opposed to 35.3% of black women have children, but never married. It was also estimated that almost 57% of families were headed by black women as opposed to 17.3% (U.S. Government Statistics) headed by white women. If these statistics are valid, the breakdown of the black family is much worse than previously feared.

If these statistics are valid, for what purpose are they being used except to show how Blacks are not constructing cohesive, value instilled family units. It is no secret that black families have gone through drastic changes since slavery. The efforts put forth to create and maintain strong family units were extremely successful before the 1960s when drugs infiltrated black communities. Strong family structures began to corrode in large numbers. Teenage childbirths escalated, welfare roles began to swell with AFDC victims of drugs and absentee fathers, and municipal welfare boomed.

This was not to be the only impact. Black males have until this day, the highest unemployment rates.

(Whites sold black family members during slavery)

Southern Whites sold slaves, and quiet as it is kept, some northern Whites did also, but more horrifying than that, they sold their own mulatto children, brothers, sisters, aunts, uncles, and cousins. Family relationship did not matter to the majority of them. If a slave owner's concubine gave birth to his child, the slave owner, in most cases, considered the child to be his property more so than his blood relative. Despite his discretionary measures, his wife and family usually knew which children were his. This resulted in extended families being sold without reservation, or a sense of kinship. His proof of non-attachment to knowledgeable family members was to sell the children. Sometimes they were sold to nearby plantation owners so the concubines could see them from time to time, but most of the time they were sold out of state.

Generation after generation, plantations grew into a rainbow of colors. Slave masters, their sons, nephews, and brothers visited the slave quarters often.

In some cases, the mulatto slaves who were permitted to stay were brought into the *big house* to care for the master and his family. They were given special privileges which further divided them from those in the slave quarters. The term *house niggers* came into use at that time. *Field nigger* was used to describe the workers from the slave quarters.

Today, there are millions of Blacks related to Whites through undeclared blood kinship. Southern Whites are the most closely related through blood kinship, and are the most racist in American culture. As long as there are Blacks of different hues in America, the white southerner is reminded of his indiscretion and appetite for mother Africa's daughters, and that appetite is still ravenous.

Because of past miscegenation, there may be more than forty thousand Blacks passing for white in America, and more throughout the world. Their reason for doing so is to escape racism.

(Black women were used by Whites during slavery)

African women brought to North America, South America, and the Caribbean served three main purposes. The first purpose was to increase the number of slaves through childbirth. This was an economical coup for slave masters. None could ask for a better commodity than one that reproduced itself.

Black male studs were forced to impregnate female slaves to increase the number of slaves on plantations, or to be sold at slave auctions. It did not matter how often a female slave gave birth as long as she reproduced she was useful. If she could not, she was placed in the fields to work, or sold off.

White slave owners offered black female slaves to white male visitors to plantations for sexual gratification as a courtesy. No reluctance was tolerated. When a female slave refused white male advances, she was publicly whipped, or sold. Sometimes her husband, children or immediate family members were sold. This served as an example to other female slaves. In time, the women learned to quietly accept their fate no matter how humiliated, dirty, and ashamed they felt. They silently let themselves be used no matter how repugnant, drunken, or filthy the intruders were. Those who did not, were killed, and sometimes maimed by their attackers.

The second purpose was the lack of compensatory servitude. The female slave could be made to toil endlessly on one plantation, or many until her death without compensation. Many worked in the fields alongside the men.

The third purpose was to nurture, care for, and protect the slave master's family. Her job in the *big house* was to serve completely. She nursed the master's babies when his wife did not. She cared for them all when they fell ill. She scrubbed their floors spotless, cooked their food, served their guests, cleaned, ironed, washed, and knew what the occupants wanted before they did. She did all this at the expense of her own family whom she rarely saw. She also felt coerced to obey the master hoping to save her children from being sold at auction.

(White men favored black women during slavery)

"No young white buck is worth his salt, if he hasn't bedded a young black wench." That was the attitude of most southern plantation owners. Their sons were encouraged to covet young virgin females in the slave quarters. "You don't have to worry about diseases if they never were had." The young men would force the young girls to submit to them. In many cases, the young man's manhood was in question if he did not force himself on young girls he had known, and played with his whole life.

Many young white males fell in love with female slaves, and never married white women. This was frowned upon by their families, but that did not matter. The plantations eventually were passed down to them, so they could spend as much time as they wanted with their concubines and children. Some of them freed their offspring, extended family members of their lovers, and even their lovers. Their lovers were often freed after the white slave owner's death if the females outlived them as in the case of President Thomas Jefferson.

White slave masters with families, who fell in love with their female concubines, sometimes freed them along with their whole families. Oftentimes, they did not. They wanted them near them at all times, and considered them personal property.

This is still prevalent today in men who claim ownership of women against their will. The desire to control women has always been a less desirable trait in men, especially white men. In European nations, it has been the custom for men to consider wives and children possessions.

Many nations adhere to such customs, but Europeans consider it their GOD given right. Connecting it to religion makes it more deadly and obsessive.

Black female slaves experienced the darkest side of the white male nature. His wife was more than willing to allow him his indiscretions if it meant she would not have to endure his malevolence. She knew what the female slave endured, and felt, "Better her than me."

(Black men were standing "at stud" during slavery)

Some of the most muscular, broadly built black male slaves were used to produce workers for slave masters. They were called up from the fields, blacksmith shops, or after tours on the fighting circuit to mate with black female slaves. They were sometimes loaned out to other plantation owners for the purpose of impregnating their female slaves.

These male slaves were not expected to have a relationship with the women bearing the children, nor any of their children. It was a rare event for a male slave to even see the children he sired. No one knows the psychological trauma this caused slaves used for this purpose, but it surely had to have a lasting impact. Is the result, the *mama's baby, papa's maybe* syndrome we see today?

Most children born in this manner were not told who their fathers were in most instances. Slave women would eventually tell their families if they knew the black slave's name. This was very important to them to keep brothers and sisters form unknowingly engaging in incestuous relationships.

Rumors circulated throughout plantations, even across state lines. Traveling preachers, fighters on the circuit, and freedmen carried tales of woe, stories of *jumpin' the broom,* which gave birth to whom and all sorts of details newspapers carry today. Escaped slaves brought back to plantations, or from other plantations also carried tales to and fro. Soon slaves began to know who was who enough to discern who gave birth and who the father was. Names were important. Names like, *"Big Jim," "Wrestlin' Willie," "Blacksmith Jack," "Black tom,"* were common.

Anonymity served the masters well, only in *their* minds. They felt only *they* knew the many secrets of their domains, when in actuality, every adult slave knowing how to keep a tight lip, knew that and more. All of the master's business was known by the slaves.

Many slave masters thought none of their slaves could read. Many slaves could read and often read documents in the master's house when they were permitted to work or enter there. Slave masters also spoke freely around them thinking they were too ignorant to understand.

(White women had their own black "studs")

Quiet as it is kept, many white women kept black male slaves as their personal love machines. They had to be more discreet about it than white males, but they enjoyed the *forbidden fruit* as much, if not more than their male counterparts.

If found out, their punishment would have been severe. It was not common for them to be put to death; they could be stripped of their clothing, horse-whipped, thrown off the land, sent away discreetly, or simply considered a wife only in terms of public appearances.

Her tactic was to force the male slave to satisfy her voracious appetite for his raw maleness. His physique appealed to her perception of male beauty. His wet black skin, glistening in the hot southern sun accenting sinewy limbs, was too tempting an invitation as she sat fanning herself, and drinking lemonade on the porch of the *big house*. His reluctance to accommodate her for fear of the slave master was overturned by her threats of rape if he did not comply. This often worked to her advantage.

The fact that she owned such a man, who would do her bidding without all the superfluous wooing, quickened her anticipation. The idea of a love slave proved too much for many a fragile and helpless damsel of purity.

Once taken, she became wantonly obsessed. Her husband's nights in the *quarters* no longer bothered her. Her jealous rages stopped, for now she understood his need for *black erotica*. He could no longer satisfy her. She sought only him. The black one. He was the only one who gave her the earthy, lusty, dusky love that moved her spirit as well as her body. The one to whom she dared not express words of love above a whisper. The one man, who could very well cause her death, gave her what she needed the most. She knew now why he was feared by white men. In him she found what they tried to hide from her. He was simply a man just like them. She found him not to be that animal white men portrayed him to be. She shared love, real love with a real man in spite of the fact that he was a slave and she basked in it.

(Blacks struggle against mental illness)

Contraindications victims suffer from racism are mental and physical illnesses. Often they are not aware of the effect built up rage has on their bodies, and personalities.

Homeless Blacks, seen on major city streets talking to themselves as if conversing with imaginary partners is indicative of what racism, impacted with life's normal ups and downs, can do. Many cannot handle the level of stress experienced, and their minds snap. Regular mind processing ceases causing them to lose control of normal mind function. Most people in society can handle life's daily stresses. However, most people do not have to deal with racist attitudes as do Blacks and other minorities. When racism is thrown into the mix, the body copes by becoming diseased physically, mentally, or both. The usual physical reactions suffered by Blacks are high blood pressure, heart disease, anxiety, exhaustion and probably many ailments not yet identifiably recognized as reactions.

The possibility of the body taking the brunt from mental trauma by becoming physically ill, thus saving the mental stability of racism's victims, should be investigated more thoroughly by black psychologists. If they *are* working on this, they are to be commended.

Depression among Blacks is prevalent. Sometimes they don't know the causes and tend to blame it on minor family, work and relationship problems. Their demeanors change instantly upon contact with negative situations, and their reactions are so far out of proportion to the incident that they question their own sanity. The blue feelings can last for various periods of time from a few seconds to months.

Since there are no sane reasons for racist treatment of Blacks, they are left with empty feelings of helplessness devoid of answers. To be disliked because of the way GOD made you, is deep. It challenges your right to exist in a world first inhabited by people of your hue. Awareness of the causes of black mental traumas is the first step to mental wellness. After all is said and done, we are hue-man.

(Whites struggle against mental illness)

Mental illness among Whites usually stems from childhood abuses more so than being oppressed by institutions and a collective group of people. Some of them may also suffer from guilt complexes for their whole race. Knowledge of historic abuses of Whites against many groups of people has left many of them feeling guilty. They know at some point the karmic debt will have to be paid. How it will happen is a mystery, and being so, they fear anyone and anything posing a threat to them and their possessions. Hence, their fears of Blacks because they are the ones done the most harm.

There are large numbers of Whites battling inner demons from past wars, inability to adapt to society's demands, or past traumatic events. The number of them suffering from schizophrenia is staggering. Medication helps to control their anti-social behavioral impulses.

White paranoia is also prevalent among masses of so-called normal Whites. They exhibit fear around blacks that they don't know. This fear is unknowingly transmitted to those around them. This fear is more controlled when Whites overwhelmingly outnumber Blacks in close quarters and in large settings.

Blacks see white fear as a guilt reflex. Whites seem to expect black retribution. Blacks chuckle at such nonsense. The only thing Blacks want from Whites is respect, and to be able to feel comfortable around them without picking up negative vibes. Everyone needs to just *chill* from the *fever* of *fear* and the insanity of *racism*.

When a race of people believe in themselves and want other races to believe in them, it is O.K. When Whites believe all races should believe and depend on them placing them above all others, they have a big problem. No matter how great Whites may perceive themselves to be, all races perceive the same about themselves. Races of people respect each other because of accomplishments and humane interaction. When Whites understand this, *we will all get along* without mental race traumas.

(Blacks embrace their culture and for the most part don't "Americanize.")

Although Blacks would like to be totally incorporated into American society, the most difficult thing to give up is their culture. They cling to it so fiercely because it is *what brought them over and through* the mean times. Without black culture, the people would have been scattered. There would be no unity, black institutions would not exist, and no means of self-identity would abound.

There must be a frame of reference in order for a people to understand self. Being locked in a place without knowledge of who one is, and where one came from, blocks one's mind as to where one is going. In fact, one doesn't know where *to* go. Blacks understood this early on, and began to build for self. Now that they are beginning to collectively know who they truly are, self-pride is moving to a higher level. There is dignity in the truth of their past. There is a majesty encompassing the mystique of their rich and brilliant ancestors. There is a joy in being Afrique because it now means beauty, regality, genius, truth, honor, and love.

Blacks need this revolutionary change of mind, quickening of heart, awakening of spirit, regeneration of soul, and opening of the *Third Eye*. It infuses self confidence, motivation, determination, and strength.

Black people are getting everything they need now during the *Renaissance* of the Age of Aquarius which is the *Age of Justice*. Why change now when being who one is *is* beauty? Why change now when the year 2009 beckons black people to realize again their greatness and glory? Why turn into something the extreme opposite of what one *is* to satisfy those in power? What about self satisfaction? Black people today are into self satisfaction like never before. They should be saluted for not deserting self to become that which has tried to destroy them.

This is why Blacks cannot dive into the *melting pot*. Their experience is like no other peoples on the planet and they know it. Other races will not let them forget that they are of a different hue. It is mirrored back to them from every aspect of their lives except in the comfort of their GOD, families and the peace within their homes.

(Whites readily give up their cultures when coming to America)

Germans, Italians, Greeks, Irish, and the remaining European strains give up their languages and customs within a few generations after having immigrated to America. The goal is to become *American*. They have little trouble diving into the melting pot to rid themselves of accents which define their identity. They want to quickly get lost in whiteness to partake of rewards only *whiteness* can bring. Examples of this shedding of identity are the many movie stars who have changed their names to conceal their European origins.

They can falsify backgrounds to move among the privileged. They can mask their identities by moving far away from family, and in some cases completely cutting themselves off from them. They can, will, and have done all manner of things to *fit in*.

"Fitting in" means money to them. They want to make money and lots of it to realize the *American Dream*. Retaining mores from the *old country* will not allow them to operate in a realm where the *Big Boys* operate. There are things they must do before they are allowed to play, however.

First of all, they have to go to the finest schools like Yale, Harvard, and Princeton. This is where they formulate networks for future advancement. They know corporations pay top dollar for their expertise and understanding of capitalistic philosophies.

Secondly, they must marry well, which means mating someone at an equal or higher level than their own. This doubles their capital and clout within the marketplace. Their children will hopefully profit from their planned moves, and elevate to an even higher echelon within society.

This is the game that is being played and with such ruthlessness and determination, that many careers and lives are destroyed because of the passion and competition involved. It used to be, *No Blacks Allowed*. Today, a few Blacks are allowed in if they fit the model of total assimilation. In case you haven't noticed, all of the acceptable ones all act and look alike.

(Black culture is necessary for black survival)

Imagine waking up one morning to find your home has been destroyed, your family gone, no one understands the language you speak, your religion is nonexistent, you are jailed, and everyone similar to you cannot understand a word you say. It's Twilight Zone time! Your whole world has been turned upside down in a blink of an eye.

The most important thing to do is to survive in spite of what has happened to you. This means learning the new language so you can understand what is expected of you. Everything around you is different than what has been the norm, so you reluctantly adjust. Incidentally, this may take many generations. You may not realize total assimilation into this new environment, but your children (if you are permitted to keep them), or grandchildren may, thus easing the debilitating stress this situation creates.

Secondly, the off-spring must eventually satisfy the innate desire to connect with the original culture which is the root of who they are. At no time can they feel complete until they know where they came from, who the indigenous people were, history of their people, and future dreams and desires of those who came before.

Thirdly, relatedness to that native culture takes place. This is essential for calling one's ancestors spirits back into equilibrium with consciousness of self. Disintegration of mind, body, and spirit no longer restricts one from looking toward the future. Prior to all three stages, the essence of self seemed nonexistent. It resided in a place unknown. It lay dormant in a void unreachable by the conscious mind because the subconscious was in a state of shock and confusion. A renewed awareness jolts everything into focus. The mind thirstily drinks in information to restore the worthiness of ego.

Appreciation for one's body develops along with self as does the spiritual renewal that usually accompanies an enlightened state of being. This is the legacy of black culture and why Blacks submerge themselves into its recesses. Culture *is* self.

(White culture demands submersion of diverse cultures into itself)

Imagine there is a country somewhere in the world where you can go to obtain everything you desire. There is one requirement before you are allowed to enter. First, you must jump into a huge vat of non-toxic liquid called the *purification process*. You are reluctant at first, but you do it in anticipation of what awaits you once you climb out.

You haven't heard of anyone dying from the experience which makes it easier for you to allow your spouse and children to also enter through the *process*. Afterward, if you are white, you feel privileged and know you have the world by the tail. All you need do now is to do all the things necessary to thrive and succeed.

You saw people of brown and black races jump into the same *purification process*, but for some reason, they were for the most part staying the same. They weren't any different than you, just a different color. They rebelled against the systematic change they were expected to adhere to. You just couldn't understand why this was happening. You were glad to get rid of your European accent, provide a decent education for your children, and interact in mainstream *processing*.

Those other people just didn't understand how this place operated. If they had done what you did, they would have reaped rewards. Everything was there for the taking. Then one day a news story hit that made you realize *those* people were not *processing* right because something in the vat infected them. You were immune to that infection.

They were infected with requirements to give up their heritage, ignore their culture and color, and psychologically embrace the supposed superiority of people looking like you. They were automatically expected in reality to do what was not required of you. The system took into consideration who you were when you were *processed,* because it was designed for you. Who they were, was ignored. The addition of fairness, equality, diversity and love added to the pot would correct the oversight. You knew it, but didn't care.

(Blacks are physically superior to Whites)

This may be true, but far be it from Blacks to use this as a means to obtain rewards in society. The superiority game has been used often enough, too often for our tastes.

Regardless of the reasons *why* Blacks have superior stamina, endurance, maneuverability, and denser bone mass, they still consider themselves equal to everyone else and want to be treated as such.

Many people believe Blacks are inferior. Extensive programming of the masses over centuries has pounded theories into the heads of us all that Blacks were lower forms of human beings. The size of skulls, brains, and facial features were used as criteria to support errant theories concocted to enhance superior feelings in Whites and inferior feelings in Blacks. All of the above theories have been proven wrong. Truth began to surface when black doctors, scientists, historians and other educated fields began questioning negative attacks on Blacks.

Further study revealed the opposite was true. It revealed that Blacks are structured exquisitely superior to all races. Their tolerance to heat surpasses all others. Their bones are denser. Their skulls are thicker. Even their blood flow is orchestrated superbly. Yet, they are not so involved with nature's gifts that they forget they must live upon the planet peacefully with others. In fact, they would rather the truth be known only to set the record straight. Further time spent on the matter is not necessary.

Diseases like diabetes, high blood pressure, and heart disease became prevalent among Blacks because of improper diets.

Africans brought to the Americas needed fresh fruits, vegetables and fish. All nourishment conducive to healthy Melanin was gleaned from the earth. Beans, fiber, nuts and grains were instrumental in sustaining them; however, these foods were not available to them. They were given pork which was the last thing they needed, but had to eat often along with other melanin clogging foods such as milk, cheese, butter, eggs, chicken, and animal fats.

(Whites struggle to compete physically with Blacks)

Quiet as it's kept, today is no different than in Roman times. Even then, Whites could not compete equally with Blacks. Whites had to exercise harder to build body mass normal to Blacks. The same is true today. They can be seen jogging, weight lifting, and running hard. Most black youth and men are naturally sinewy. Do your own comparisons. Average fifteen-year-old boys standing side by side from each race, none having had weight or athletic training will bear this out. Supporters of white supremacy will quickly say slavery caused the superior development in black males. If we look at Africans, we will find the same physical attributes. Oops, there it is!

Not too many years ago Blacks were not allowed to participate in professional sports because they were considered mentally and physically inferior. Whites can hardly find a place on teams because of the superior play of Blacks. Oh yes, the number of black quarterbacks is growing steadily. Basketball has gone the way of football. One has to look hard in order to find a white face nowadays. Black coaches and managers are also proving their worth.

Sports less inhabited by Blacks is swimming, auto racing, bicycle racing, hockey, and ice skating. As soon as black youth gain exposure to these sports within community facilities, they will begin to excel in them also. It's just a matter of time. Even golf is no longer a white bastion. Tiger Woods has seen to that.

This leaves white athletes little room to excel. Many have moved into management and sports announcing, or joined foreign leagues. Not far behind them are a slew of Blacks with like aspirations. Because of the infiltration of Blacks, new sports Whites can excel in are being added to the Olympics roster.

Why do they run? Why do they *have* to be superior? When they are proven less capable, why do they continue the farce with superior attitudes? Blacks have arrived, and Whites are saddened to see their favorite fantasy disappearing before their eyes.

(Blacks understand the divide and conquer philosophy of Whites)

Some Blacks play the game to their advantage and others do not. *The game* is to undercut each other, or just about anyone in order to attain a goal that is dangled before them. This game is not exclusive to Blacks, anyone can play. If exclusivity belongs to any group, it would have to be claimed by the creators of the game, white Europeans.

When there is an adversary or quest for *some thing* and there is a group barring the way, the group must be divided in some way in order for conquest to be made. One person can be swayed to betray the group by any means necessary. People can infiltrate and be used to investigate the weaknesses of the group, persons from the group can be used to distract the group from its focal point, the group can be deceived about its leadership, or the leadership can be misguided in making decisions for the group which in turn causes dissention within the group.

Blacks know these games well. They have been used against them and Native Americans for centuries. In the past, there was no power within the group to withstand the pressure put upon it. Today knowledge of such tactics is sweet, but application of that knowledge with wisdom is sweeter. Blacks must take inventory on what has been learned, apply it wisely, and never again let the weapons of dissention successfully divide them.

Those Blacks willing to *sell out* should be exposed. They are opportunists at ready to sacrifice the group for self-aggrandizement, money, power, and influence. Some would do so for love and appreciation from those seeking to control or destroy their people.

If Blacks are to again be subjugated let it not be because they were caught unawares by the same tactics used in the past.

The Willie Lynch philosophy has bode well for Whites when dealing with the slave mentality of some Blacks. The course he directed them on has kept not only Blacks but all groups under their rule to be controlled by them psychologically. No fears from the body when the mind is under complete control. Breaking away from mind control means freedom.

Of what use is knowledge, if not utilized?
Of what benefit is wisdom, if not applied?

(Whites are comfortable in the divide and conquer mode)

Unity is the most devastated element in the *divide and conquer* scheme. Where there is unity, no division can take place. Where there is no division, there is no *inlet* for an adversary to infiltrate, operate, indoctrinate, or subjugate.

Throughout history Europeans have used the tactic of divide and conquer among peoples unaware of such human debauchery. A simple people, content living on their piece of *the rock*, unfettered by dreams of world domination and subjugation of others, were herded like cattle, and in most cases murdered for their land, resources, women and possessions. The song was played over and over again until the world was laid bare of its innocence before the feet of the *pale horsemen*.

Games are still being played by the same people today. New generations of peoples defeated have forgotten the plight of their forefathers, or have joined their oppressors in acknowledgement of that defeat. They believe there is no winning against a foe capable of the worse inhumanity that the earth has ever known. The comfort exhibited in this mode daily by Whites, be it in business, entertainment, sports, or international affairs, is disheartening. They destroy lives and say, *"it's not personal. It's just business."* They undercut careers for self gain and say, *"only the strong survive in this game."* They take a life, and without remorse say, *"it was an accident,"* and behind closed doors say the person deserved it. They are constantly bettering the odds of their success by destroying that of others.

Not all Whites are good at this game, but most of them play it. Some wouldn't dare do dishonest things to others. They live simple every day lives, and are content with what they have. The majority will do anything, and are never content without a large slice of the pie. If they see it in someone else's hands, they will surely jockey themselves into position to topple it into their own.

Now that the economy slowed and everyone has taken a severe hit financially, some people have given up hope of recouping what was lost and others are gearing up to use drastic measures in response to these drastic times to acquire what was lost.

(Blacks (some) imitate white behavior)

Black people know many Blacks with a strong compulsion to be white. They mimic white behavior in every area of their lives. They act, dress, display characteristics and mannerisms, only attend white establishments, date Whites only, express dislike for or hatred of Blacks, and do not associate with Blacks.

Every black person knows, or has heard of someone who has decided to *cross over*. These are not people crossing over because they look white. To the contrary, many are *exceptionally* dark complexioned individuals. They cross over because they are either ashamed of being black or think being black means they are inferior to Whites. They begin by dressing exclusively in white designer fashions. They would not be caught in anything considered typical African garb.

They begin to act white, and display white characteristics. Blacks do not need that to be explained. For those unaware, it is simple. There is a difference in the way black people culturally relate to each other in comparison to Whites. You know the valley girl personality Whoopi Goldberg mimic? Well, they begin to display that type of persona. They know Whites find this behavior acceptable. They study Whites carefully in order to pull it off.

Next, they hang out at all white establishments in order to introduce themselves to Whites with whom they wish to ingratiate themselves. Once this has been established, they are ready for the next step.

They begin to vocalize their dislike of other Blacks, and refuse to associate with them. They think they have finally made it into whiteness. Whites actually pity their self-hatred, and begin to use them. They are agreeable pawns. They allow themselves to be used completely in the service of those whom they think will add to their advancement and secure their futures. By the time they understand that they trust people who will throw them under the bus if and when the need arises, it is too late.

(Whites accept Blacks who imitate them)

Blacks vying for white acceptance within exclusively white environments, think they are welcomed when treated in a way they assume is equal. They have purposely brainwashed themselves. They have done everything humanly possible to superficially transform themselves into someone different. Regrettably, these are the Blacks most accepted by Whites. Although the number of Blacks choosing this course is unknown, whatever the number, it is unacceptable behavior to black people with pride in their heritage.

Some Whites may find associating with Blacks socially amusing for a while, but true friendship is built on sturdier stuff. This is not to say some do not value Blacks as true friends, but relationships built on trust, healthy self images, and shared experiences cannot become a reality if Blacks do not value themselves.

There are many Blacks sharing positive friendships with Whites. Some do not have to change themselves in any way, in order to develop the relationships. They brought who they were into the equation and was accepted, respected, and loved for it. This type of connection allows Whites an opportunity to understand the view from the other *side*. Blacks caught up in becoming what they are not, missed and are missing this rewarding experience.

Many whites do not care for pseudo Whites.

They are more fascinated with Blacks in African garb. They admire black hair styles (and will comment on them), and jewelry. This provides them the adventure, and stimulation they constantly seek for something different. They just can't get past the skin color to communicate equally. It is too vast an extreme for them to fathom. They are paranoid, uncertain of their reactions, and do not want to fraternize.

They also do not know where to draw the line and fear causing negative reactions from Blacks. Their tactic is to just go along with the status quo. Just leave things as they are.

(Blacks deal with white hostility on a daily basis)

Wherever Blacks go, and whatever they do, if Whites are involved or present, there is bound to be some level of hostility evident. Whites have a tendency through their speech, eye contact (or lack of it), and their deeds to let Blacks know they have disdain for them.

Some Whites seem to look at Blacks as though they are wondering, *"Why are you here? Why don't you go some place else?"* they seem to draw pleasure from making Blacks feel uncomfortable. Actually, it could very well be they feel uncomfortable whenever Blacks are around and try to shift it off themselves onto others. Do they fear Blacks so much that they have to show hostility to hide it?

Not all Whites give off this abrasiveness. There are regular people with correct civil behavior, but to run into one of them seems to be few and far between. It makes one feel there's hope whenever one of them are around. That's why white native New Yorkers (excluding places like Benson Hurst, of course) are such likeable people. They are sophisticated enough to wheel and deal on a level most Americans know little about. *"You don't have to be my friend, just show me proper respect and be civil, and we can get along."*

The rage building up in blacks would ease if white America would just *chill out* and just act as natural plain folks. Both races have been in this country together long enough to at least tolerate each other on a less hostile level.

Blacks would become more likeable toward Whites if Whites would **stop** staring at them like they are an oddity when frequenting exclusive restaurants (the whole place becomes quiet), being so nervous around Blacks, assuming all Blacks are criminals, anticipating reactions, making stupid racial statements, stereotyping all black people, assuming all black men are criminals, calling black women *girl* and *gal,* calling black men *boy,* saying *you people,* saying the *"N" word,* hurting black children's feelings by not permitting children to play together and so many other debasements.

(Whites (some) live in an America that is alien to most Blacks)

The vision of life in America is obviously different for people of various groups. This space we all share is often described by Whites as a wonderful place to rear children with wonderful school systems. Some people would wonder what country they are talking about.

Beautiful homes line suburban streets with manicured lawns tended by lawn services. Two to four luxury cars in front of homes big enough to house a small army are countless in number. The homes are filled with the latest electronic gadgets, and everything anyone would hope to use or need. Backyards with pools the length of the homes are commonplace. This is suburban America. There are Blacks sprinkled throughout (if allowed in), but the majority of residents in upper crust areas are white.

They experience a lifestyle of living most minorities have never experienced and probably never will. They have no contact with people outside their economic circle and would rather not, *thank you*. Some still believe all Americans can have all the *things* they possess with *just a little ingenuity and hard work*. These people have profited the most, cared, and given the least. Their world is what America is to them. Anyone else's version of anything less than that is *poppycock*.

Their world is filled with clubs, horse and dog shows, Jennifer's dancing lessons, and Winifred's equestrian lessons. Their main concern is what's going on in the financial world, their social register, and with their society friends (Jet Set). They are different than middle and upper middle class Whites.

The average white family is concerned with accumulation and maintaining what they have. Basic survival on a daily basis is not their concern. When their world changes through divorce, death of a spouse, or job loss leaving them penniless, the *"I can identify with your pain"* becomes real for them. Now they can see the bottom from where they are.

Life changes drastically and they may be relocated next door to people whom they never would have thought they would be exposed. Now what are you going to do? You can love your neighbor, or hate them. Love is better.

(Black youth speak a language unto themselves)

Sometimes you can be around teenagers and not understand what is being said. Words are used in the most illogical forms imaginable. They say things like, *word up*. You keep listening for meaning, and feel like a complete fool because somewhere you got lost in the shuffle and language zoomed right into the twenty first century without you having the vaguest idea where it was going. You can't listen in on their conversations. You need a slang dictionary (created by them) to decipher it.

Black youth have a language like that. It is like a patois, yet it is not. It's like slang, but it isn't. It's like broken English, but it goes way beyond that. It's like, well, you know, it's...it's *just like that*. There's no explanation for it. It just is. Some Blacks understand it. Those who don't understand have been away from the *hood* for so long, they have lost an *ear for* it. Some of those in the hood never developed an ear *for* it.

I'm not getting into the ain'ts and double negatives here. I'm speaking *close you out of the mix* stuff here. Just listen to the rappers. Can you figure it out? Being black doesn't qualify you to speak the language. You have got to be *dope* to understand the evolution of it from *Jump Street*. When the speakers want to let you in, they relax the *vibe* so you can enter. When they tire of you, you're shut out.

The black community has Black English also. It is the last vestige of slavery. It symbolizes the difficult attempt on the part of Blacks to learn a language totally obscene to the African ear and tongue. Obscene in the sense that no language more complicated in essence of meaning, and delivery of speech challenged the African more than English after Whites forbade him to speak his mother tongue.

Lack of a frame of reference stunted his growth in understanding the language. No schools taught him the use of words. Survival alone forced him to understand what he could, and what he could not, he made up. The result is Black English.

(Whites want everyone to speak their language)

All cultures come to America with languages unique unto themselves. They jump into the *pool of forgetfulness* (melting pot) to become what they consider to be a *true American*. While bathing in this pool, foreign languages are discarded. Dialects are sometimes held onto until a certain level of comfort is reached speaking American English.

Many white Americans (living in America two generations or longer) look upon non-English speaking peoples (usually minorities) living in the United States with a jaundiced eye. They vilify them on talk radio, in the news, and refuse to consider them for various types of employment. There is definitely coercion going on against non-English speaking people.

Many minorities immigrating to America speak their native languages. Learning English is a monumental task at best. They strive to do so at a pace that is slow, but comfortable for them. Until they have full command of the language, it is unfair to refuse them the same rights and privileges of other Americans when they have taken the time and effort to become citizens of this country. They do speak English, but not at everyone else's pace. A functional grasp should be acceptable until they are fully articulate in the language. Everyone *should* communicate with everyone else in order for the system to function adequately. After having learned English, however, whatever language they choose to speak outside of their jobs is their own affair. No one should be coerced into giving up their native tongue or culture because others are uncomfortable with them.

Since Whites have chosen to give up native cultures and languages from their originating countries, some of them feel everyone else must make the same sacrifice. The difference is lost on other peoples not having shameful pasts. They love the history of their people. They cherish their ancestor's accomplishments. They do not feel the need to distance themselves from those cultures. They have no need to change, but will to do so because it is required and a necessary evil.

(Blacks are too paranoid of Whites)

There are a great many Blacks paranoid of Whites, and with good reason. Throughout the years, since slavery, some Whites have used coercive methods to instill fear in Black men and women. They have used the threat of lowered pay, unemployment, beatings, killings, rapes, and every subtle conniving tactic open to them to control the behavior of black people. If the desired behavior was not exhibited, they felt compelled to act on those threats, and did. They still do today.

 People unfamiliar with the unique black/white relationship in America cannot begin to understand it until they seriously sift through the deep abyss of anguish, abhorrence, and division Whites created in order to utilize black brawn and creativity for economic purposes.

Other cultures now embracing America's shores see only the surface of a four-hundred-year tie that has bound the two into a gruesome partnership built on an ugly, demonic, and unresolved foundation of iniquity and distrust.

Black paranoia should be rampant considering past abuses. The fact that it isn't, bodes well for the victims. They alone have bandaged the wounds on their hearts and souls. They alone have psychologically patched themselves up in order to function. They alone have reached into their souls to do as *their* GOD taught, to: love *those that do all manner of evil against you."* They along with their Native American brothers and sisters have foraged through this maze of unknown strategies used to repel them backwards. Like their Jewish brother who wishes an end to all *this slavery stuff,* they cannot forget what happened, and with greater cause.

Black paranoia is different today than in the past. Fear of being isolated among Whites may deter many Blacks from achieving their full potential. White's past history of broken promises does not bode well for them. Blacks are learning to build for self without dependence on others.

Having felt the sting of the wasp; would one return to disturb the nest?

(Whites are afraid of Blacks)

On a radio talk show, this author was asked, *"Why do you say Whites fear Blacks?"* the answer was succinct, *"Whites fear retribution for all the wrongs they know they have done to Blacks."*

Black people are not an aggressive, vengeful people. They have always been open to reconciliation, compromise, and agreeable settling of past scores. It is Whites who refuse to compromise at the bargaining table. Their greed has crippled them. Their fear actually stems from their own conscious knowledge that nature always balances the scales.

Some Whites would cringe at the notion of fearing anyone. Yet, when Affirmative Action or reparations is mentioned, they immediately display apprehensive behavior. *"Blacks are taking our jobs." "We can't afford to pay Blacks for slavery." "The constitution doesn't allow for it." "Why do we have to give them anything?" "We work hard for what we have." "Why can't they do what we did? Work for it."*

They also display their fear when among Blacks. Their demeanor changes. They try to act *cool,* walk *hip,* talk *hip,* label their youth *Wiggers,* and use vernacular they're unaccustomed to. They begin to perspire, get clammy hands, look around constantly, clasp their bags and purses, and try not to have eye contact. All the signs are there, and Blacks make note of them. This behavior makes some Blacks uncomfortable because they know there is no reason for such fears.

Other Blacks may feel a sense of power, and find the whole scenario amusing. The criminal element will surely see such people as prey. Admitting what is evident within a society is half the battle. Solving the problems of what is known within a society is the other half. Unless both sides of this equation are willing to realistically deal with problems by each opening up Pandora's Box, there is little hope for, ***one nation, indivisible, with liberty and justice for all.***

(Blacks, finding themselves in predominately white surroundings, feel isolated)

One of the worst feelings imaginable is suddenly finding oneself in a place where all eyes are on you while pretending not to be. One feels singled out, preyed upon, and invaded. Trepidation slowly causes arm hairs to stand on end, palms to sweat, neck hairs to tingle, and the uneasiness may make the person want to leave.

What has just been described, is the feeling most Blacks feel when in predominately white surroundings with strangers. The place is not important. It could be a supermarket, restaurant, freeway, office, strange neighborhood, school, or bar. This is a normal happening for Blacks. Blacks in mainstream America are most often surrounded by Whites. This means they are most often caught up in an alien environment with people who are uncomfortable with them being there.

Not all Blacks feel this way. There are some who feel comfortable around Whites only. Usually they have shared an environment with Whites, and know them well enough to *put on the face* for them. *Wearing the mask* is simply being the type of black one knows Whites do not feel intimidated by. It's in the speech, demeanor, and walk. In other words, it's imitating them. The more a black acts like them, the more they accept him. He is one of the programmed ones. The others are considered to be unpredictable.

There was a time when black men would not let themselves wander into exclusively white environments, especially if white women were present. Black males would be beaten, or lynched for looking at white women, whether they were guilty, or not. Black men had to hold their heads down to assure Whites they were not *eyeballing* them.

There is much history in the relationship between Blacks and Whites that is unhealthy and deadly. Now is the time for all of us to face each other squarely, deal with our disagreements, forgive past sins, compensate for past deeds and offer each other love. Its time to move on together to create a model society that GOD can look down upon and say, *"These are my children of whom I am well pleased."*

(Whites finding themselves in predominately black surroundings, feel intimidated)

Some Whites finding themselves in totally black environments feel uncomfortable, fearful, and distrustful of everyone around them. If they must ask someone for information, they will look for the most vulnerable looking person available. Usually, it's a woman. They tend to have less fear and distrust if they have been exposed to Blacks for long periods of time. If not, they do not know what to expect. All the false stereotypical tapes come to life in their minds like a Peter Pan movie. They imagine being brutalized, raped, robbed, beaten, and killed by a mindless group of animals. When their expectations are not realized, they either feel it was because they took control of the situation (when they really didn't), or they were lucky enough to not run into *those kind of Blacks,* rather than assume the area was safe.

The reason for their fears is lack of correct information. The information they have is slanted. A catastrophic event has to take place before they realize their error in judgment. Many incidents that have occurred where Blacks have died saving or trying to save the lives of Whites because the Whites thought they meant them harm.

The black community is protective of itself and anyone coming into it. Usually the way Whites act may cause them to become prey to elements seeking vulnerable persons no matter *what* color they are.

Whites do some ridiculous things when they find themselves around Blacks. They flash money as if they are the masters of the world. That's a no-no in any community, especially where people are destitute. They start off with *you people,* progress to *"I love black people,"* and if drinking, want to claim a black stranger as their best friend.

The tour buses entering Harlem are full of them. They leave their buses in groups, and walk around gaping at Blacks as if they are seeing them for the first time. It's hilarious to some Blacks, and resented by others.

It's not safe for Blacks to tour white neighborhoods!

(Black's earthy quality unnerves Whites)

Blacks moving their heads while speaking, using hand motions, snapping fingers, waving arms, and other movements of expression while talking to Whites, makes many Whites feel uncomfortable. They are not used to the flamboyant style that originated in Africa, and is served up in minority communities with black populations.

Many Whites do not know how to deal with the informality of it all. They would rather have polite impersonal, superficial conversations on the job, and during casual meetings. They don't know how, nor do they want to *get down* and *be for real*. They want distance.

Blacks have the tendency to come close to you when they talk to you. It is an *"in your face"* thing. That is no accident. Blacks originally come from warm climates that are conducive to a warm people. To get close, is to bond with another person in language, auras, physically, and emotionally. Warmth is the key word here. Whites are not used to this kind of communication unless they have had close contacts with Blacks, or other warm groups of people.

The mere earthiness of black people shows their connection with that from which they came. There is no pretense (in most cases). *"It is what it is."* There is no superficiality. *"What you see is what you get."* (Again, in most cases.) There is no lack of understanding, because we're talking about *"The real deal."*

All earthiness is not slang. It can be regular conversation. It is not only what is said, but how it is said. The tonal quality of the voice puts one in touch with how sincere, sure, truthful, and determined the speaker may be. The way it is said adds to it.

Some white youth are catching on. They are digging deep to feel what they say, rather than just saying words. Language is expressive. Bodies are instruments of expression. Blacks and other peoples of color are expressive beings using all of their equipment to get messages across. Italians, the French, and Spaniards show their Africoid mannerisms daily.

(Whites have a problem dealing with black "attitude.")

People express themselves in many ways. Orientals are known to be quiet and reserved. Asians can become quite animated and become excited to the point that no one understands what they are saying. Italians are quite expressive with their hands. Hispanics tend to speak quickly, and use facial expressions more so than others. Blacks are known for having a certain *attitude* when expressing themselves.

Many Whites have a problem with all of the above modes of behavior. The ones that seem to disturb them the most are the behaviors displayed by Orientals and Blacks.

Orientals do not show how they feel in general, or what they think in their expressions that oftentimes perplex Whites. Blacks on the other hand, are too expressive. They show too much expression in the form of an *attitude*. They appear to be challenging the white person. This is not the case, but it is taken as such. Whites mistake a mode of expression as a challenge to their authority. This they cannot tolerate. They feel they are superior and should be given superior respect.

Many Whites assume Blacks are envious of their positions, resent being told what to do and the show of *attitude* is a sign of disrespect. Actually, it is simply Blacks expressing themselves the way they do at home, or anywhere else. To Blacks, it is just being themselves. To Whites, it is considered insubordination. Many jobs have been lost due to miscommunications of this type. This is why Whites want minorities to speak their language. They want to be sure they understand the messages being sent to them in their language, and on their terms. When it is not, they become paranoid.

Black females have plenty of *attitude*. All of them have natural rhythm, but some have overprotective natures. They are always on guard around Whites. The past has created this trait of survival defensiveness that will remain until it is no longer needed. Although it has hurt many Blacks in the marketplace, it has done more good than harm. It has kept many Blacks alive.

Conclusion

It's amazing how different people see things differently, especially Blacks and Whites. When an historic evaluation is done, reasons for differences become quite clear. These two groups have had totally different experiences while occupying the same space in time and location. Neither understood the impact it would eventually have on them as individuals, and each within his group. More than four hundred years have elapsed with moderate change in their relationship.

Changes in laws, physical association within society, and efforts made to try to understand each other have been hopeful. Fearful men within the majority group, however, continuously circumvent these advances.

Majority group resentment of minority group progress keeps the two separate, and unequal. No matter how powerful the majority considers itself to be, it is always aware of challenges to its authority and right to rule over others. No one has better right to challenge that than those having felt the brunt of power wielded wildly and maniacally over a long period of time.

This relationship has been a tenuous one. It borders on kinship so strong, no other group may interfere. Bloodlines tighten the bond to the breaking point. So vastly different are they, yet they are one. As day is to night, and good is to bad, so they wander aimlessly one waiting on the other to give in as night must give into day, and day must relinquish its hold on light.

Their forefathers and foremothers mingled blood one with the other creating a rainbow of hue possibly in hopes of uniting them forever. Is the river between them too deep and the valley too wide? All efforts made by the few have fallen on deaf ears and hardened hearts. The infancy of their relationship has matured, and catapulted them into today's adolescence. They must now choose together which direction their love-hate relationship will go. Will it continue festering in the sea of inactivity, grow, or will it die?

Chapter Four

Black Men, White Women, Black Women, White Men

(Black women want white men for a number of reasons)

Some black women want white men because they believe they adore and respect women of color. They think white men admire their beauty, strength, rhythm, and sensitivity. Others may want and need someone to take care of them, and protect them. They may want to live in safe neighborhoods with mixed couples like themselves. Some may want to have children with a better chance of *making it* in the world as it is today. They know white men are the controllers, so they want to be included in their lifestyle instead of the one the sisters know and abhor.

Some sisters want their children to have long, flowing *fine hair, straight noses, and light skin*. They are more *acceptable* to the ruling class than dark-skinned children. They overly protect their children because they are *different* from other Blacks. They are *special*. Only the best schools, companions, and activities are chosen for them. They have transformed their existence for the *have-nots* into the *haves*. They will make sure their children associate with Whites only (in many cases). This way, the assimilation process may continue through them.

Some black women can't find eligible black men to marry. It seems *"all the good ones are either married, or gay. The rest of them are in jail, on drugs, or not hittin' a lick on a stick."* The black men they might consider marrying are hard to find, or seem to be *stuck on themselves*. So these women begin to look elsewhere for mates. For these women, color lines may be dropped due to necessity, not necessarily preference.

Some sisters want financial security, and want to live the *good life*. White men can provide them and their children with the *finer* things in life that they believe a black man cannot.

They fell in love.

(White men want a black woman for a number of reasons)

Some reasons might be her *attitude*, style, strength, and rhythm. Many white men have said, *"She's just unique."* There's not much difference in the average white women, but black women have a certain flair and coolness about them. They have *attitude*.

Another reason white men are drawn to black women is the need to protect someone less fortunate than themselves. Some of these men are truly liberal in their thinking, and want to feel assured of their commitment to equality.

Others want to create a child of color, and can only accomplish their goal with a woman of color (Dr. Frances Cress Welsing's theory). Being honorable men, they marry the women, produce children, and provide for their families as comfortably as possible.

Some white men prefer the earthiness of black women. They don't feel intimidated by strong women, and, in fact, prefer a woman as strong as themselves. They know she can take care of herself without needing him around to control the situation.

Some white men are fascinated by the complete opposite of themselves. *Forbidden fruit* is the only fruit they choose to sample. They do not fight the urge to approach women of color, nor do they adhere to social norms created by other Whites to keep them away from the *chocolate ladies*.

Black women do not constantly badger white men to climb the ladder of success. It is within the female's interest to let the men operate in the white world alone. The men know it best, and can move at their own pace through it. He often leaves her to her own devices as well concerning employment, if he allows her to work.

If they are influential, they can assist the women in succeeding in the marketplace.

Another reason a white man may want to romance and marry a black woman is because he fell in love.

(Black men date, live with, and marry white women for many reasons)

One reason is the *fabulous white thigh* syndrome. There aren't many chances for black men to meet and date a variety of white women in black communities. The media holds her in such high esteem, in regard to her beauty and poise, that some black men become attracted to her. Some of them feel a need to flaunt her in front of white men knowing the pairing incenses them.

Another reason is hatred of self. Rather than produce children that are like him, he would rather give his kids *a break* by giving them *fine hair,* and *a light complexion.*

Some black men mistreat white women. This is their way of retaliating for perceived past systemic injustices. They seek to control them completely. Their repugnance of all that has been done to them is reflected in the way they treat them. Someone has to pay so they choose the image that is closest to the perceived enemy.

Advancement may be another reason they latch onto a successful white woman. Her influence and connections might enable him to rise within the company, or system.

This is not the norm. Usually a black man will choose a homely white woman. This seems strange. If the same men were to choose black women, they would normally select the best looking sisters in town. When they choose white, it doesn't seem to matter what she looks like, as long as she's white. There must be some psychological meaning in this. It is certainly unsettling to black women.

Curiosity of the extreme opposite of self is another reason for the choice. Could this be what Spike Lee called *Jungle Fever?* Whatever it is, it sure aggravates some black women.

The last, but not least of all reasons for the connection is *love.* He finally met someone who totally understands him, caters to him, and treats him like a *real man.* He likes her style. It has absolutely nothing to do with race. She simply *turns him on.*

(White women want a black man for a number of reasons)

One reason may be his sexual prowess. She sees a man that intrigues her. There is a mystery about him that fascinates her. She wants to be possessed by this man that white men have been telling her all her life to stay away from. What is it that they are afraid she might find out? One thing she has heard is that black men are more endowed than many white men. She decides to do her own investigation.

Black men have a macho type of dogged determination about them that is hard for her to ignore. They walk differently than white men, and they talk in smooth lyrical almost poetic ways when trying to woo her. She can't just brush them off. They are persistent and confident they can have her, and usually they're right.

Some white women may just want a plaything with all the equipment needed to play the games she likes to play. Her money may buy him for her. This is a mutual exchange between them. She gives him money, and he satisfies her needs.

Some white women want to create color, and the only way to do that is to give birth to a black man's baby.

She may want to prove she *doesn't have* a *racist bone in her body* when challenged by a black man who may be macking her. His intention is to conquer her, her intention is to ward him off. His accusation of color bias makes her feel she must prove her point, so she sleeps with him, likes it, and continues on a long-term basis.

She is attracted to the extreme opposite to herself (*Jungle Fever) or,* she's in love with another human being that just happens to be black.

In 2008, integrated couples are a growing minority. The turned heads, looks of disdain and snide remarks do little to deter them from choosing, living with or marrying anyone they desire regardless of skin pigmentation.

(Black women are acceptable to black men when imitating white women)

This seems to be a truthful statement when we look at the black women most often approached by black men. They usually have perms and weaves. The result is long flowing straight hair. That which was not the hair all of them were born with. That doesn't mean there are no sisters with naturally long flowing straight hair. All kinds of hair are in the race. They are excluded from this analysis. The ones born with *naps* have suffered real *pain* getting that hair just right for the brothers. Why?

Why is it that most black men want black women to have that *white* look? Has self hatred brought Blacks to the point where they have fallen for the *hype* of what is truly beautiful? Has the image force-fed to them for so many years become *their* gauge for how Blacks view themselves?" Let's hope not. There is nothing more beautiful than a woman in her natural state. If she selects dreads, that is her natural beauty. Afros appeal to many, and accentuate those finely chiseled cheekbones. Braids bring out the natural beauty in many sisters aspiring to remain true to the original woman.

After all the changes made by sisters, brothers still cannot get that white image out of their minds. If a sister hasn't straightened out the kinks, some brothers can't adjust. Thank GOD all brothers aren't brainwashed. If they were, sisters would all end up by themselves or with white men or other men of various nationalities who appreciate women of a darker hue, **and their hair!**

Black women of today are as diverse as flowers. There are so many types and flavors of them. Self-pride is never absent from their demeanors as they stride as confident ornamented regal queens.

"We, as black women now pledge to be true to self, to love our natural beauty, enhance ourselves with natural African apparel, and ignore brothers unappreciative of our Godly gifts. We are beauty. We are unique. We are God's jewels."

(Whites see black women as imitations of white women)

Odd as it may seem, when some Whites see black women with straight hair, they actually believe black women are imitating them. They know the texture of black hair, and in many cases wonder why Blacks cook their hair to make it appear like theirs. The efforts Whites use to frizz their hair are rarely successful.

They also question why some Blacks use skin bleaching creams while they strive so hard to tan theirs. As far as they are concerned, everything they see as beautiful in Blacks, many Blacks are trying to change. What they do not understand is that skin bleaches may be used by many Blacks to cover flaws in melanin discoloration that may occur in black skin tones.

Many white women see the rainbow of black women as a beautiful mosaic and fear the loss of their men to *them*. The mysterious black woman has always fascinated white men, and white women know it.

Many educated Whites also understand the psychological need of the oppressed to identify with the oppressor. The need to feel valued can cause one to deny self by becoming one with the powerful oppressor by mimicking them. This need is displayed by the oppressed taking on the characteristics of the oppressor. People exhibiting this behavior in most cases are unaware of what motivates them to act this way. When they are informed of this psychological process, denial, or defensive reactions kick in. There is no hiding place from truth. Once it has been revealed, they will eventually have to acknowledge it within themselves.

Since we have to admit that some black women *are* satisfied clones of white women, we can only observe and keep trying to educate them. Once minds are convinced to deal with an immovable force for the purpose of self-preservation and that course has proven successful, no amount of counsel will convince them to change. That is the challenge we face with them.

As long as the mind is in tact, and self-love exists within the majority of Blacks, we will have to endure the last vestiges of mental slavery still existent in American society.

(Black Sisterhood)

"I have never wished I was a man no matter how sexist the society, Why? It's simple. I wouldn't want to have to compete with someone like me. I am awesome as a woman."

Black sisterhood is not a club that women can join. They automatically become members at birth. The membership is for life regardless of choice. Parentage and physical features alert others to group affiliation. What does this mean? If a woman appears to be of African heritage, she is considered black by everyone she comes into contact with in this society. There is no birth certificate needed, nor wanted to clarify mixed parentage. If she looks black, she is. It is important for people in America to categorize her as they do others. Once identified and categorized, she is dealt with accordingly. The only escape for her is to appear to be what she is not. If she appears white, she can cross over, if not, she remains in the club. Some women find the club taxing and crossover easily.

This club is unique. Women of African heritage have qualities beyond those found in women outside the club. They are strong mentally and physically, spiritual, earthy, rhythmic, comedic, and just as mysterious as their darkness implies. They are challenging, nurturing, protective, enduring, patient, and tolerant. These women possess these qualities because nature endowed them with what is still needed to survive on earth.

Every woman in this club sees herself in her sister's eyes. She sees her torment, feels her pain, understands her anxieties, knows her anguish, and shares her heartache over love gone astray. Not every woman realizes great pain in this life, but she can understand it. Not all have loved and lost, but they can sympathize. The exclusivity of this club is the hardship it presents its members, which strengthens them.

The good news is that they know if they respect, acknowledge, appreciate, protect, guide, love, and embrace each other, no man can come between them and each will give and take only what is hers.

(White Sisterhood)

The uniqueness of this club also depends on appearance. Their appearance affords them opportunities not given Black Sisterhood, but still does not eliminate them from pain. White skin is the only requirement. There is one glitch, however. There are two classes within the ranks. One class is exclusively upper crust, while the other is beneath them. All members are not afforded the same respect. Among the lower class are categorizations such as; poverty stricken, immoral, extremist, suffrage, sexual deviant, uneducated, and what they label *poor white trash*.

The rulers within society protect members of the club. They are also abused by the same. They reap rewards if they are subservient to the wishes of their men. They are used at the whim of men, confident in their hold over them financially and physically.

Many of them have abdicated to men of other races to escape maltreatment, or were attracted by attributes not common among white men. They have found this no escape from pain. They do it because they know this is the greatest insult to white men egoistically inclined to believe in their own superiority, and for personal reasons.

This club of women is strong, confident, understanding of pain common to all females, persistent, and can be supportive of others unlike themselves. Some of them are not sympathetic to causes not linked to their own. Those who are, operate outside the club, and are demeaned for it.

This club's members are as varied as the countries from which their fore parents immigrated. If hardships were experienced, they are more prone to identify with the pain of others regardless of race. Many have been of great service and inspiration to society because of their fairness, fearlessness, and the ability to stand for what is right. Many members sacrifice club unity for justice and equality. An example of such great strength was Eleanor Roosevelt.

When inequality was the norm Eleanor Roosevelt stood her ground and fought for the rights of all people. She used her rank as First Lady to defy the powerful and educate the ignorant.

(Black women have been the strength of the race)

Black women have gone to hell and back for their people. They have sacrificed their minds, bodies, souls, lives, pride, beauty, and even their dreams for the survival of black men and children. They have given full measure, and asked only for it to not have been in vain. Today's black women are still giving their all, and they will be damned if it all goes for naught. The struggle has been too hard, too lean, and too mean for too long.

Since there is no need to strive for anti-lynching laws; she feels her people have evolved to the point where the focus should be on self-evaluation, self-determination, self-dependency, and economic self-growth. Every time she lets go of one struggle, low and behold, there's another one brewing. She can't rest just yet.

The powers that be are attacking Affirmative Action. They are also trying to use the law to punish poor children for the sins of their parents. They want to take the money saved, give it to those not worthy of it, and then say the same people will create jobs with it. She knows this isn't so, because when they decided on NAFTA years ago the jobs were sent out of the country. Where are the new jobs? She must encourage her people to become entrepreneurs. She must vote for green construction to preserve the earth if her children are going to have jobs in this country. She has to see the world through international eyes just to stay grounded in what's happening now that impacts on the future of her people.

Black women have always been the obvious strength of the race. They have been allowed to maneuver where black men are not permitted to tread. They have taken liberties even white women dare not take. The black woman has mothered the planet, and weeps for her ill-fated white children who have become strangers to her and do not acknowledge her. She grieves for her children of color suffering affliction under their thumb. She knows she must be the patient, nurturing, guiding force to bring them together. But how long must she wait?

The black woman is God's gift of love and patience to the world

(Whites think black men are the strength of the race)

Black men are indeed strong. They have been responsible for building most of America during and after slavery. Their physical strength should never be underestimated. Whites see their strength as the foundation of black strength. They perceive male strength to be physical; therefore it must be subdued in order to subdue black people collectively.

Black males have not been allowed total mobility within American society because of this main factor (not excluding pursuing the white female, of course). He has been contained psychologically, emotionally, and physically and he *knows* it. His limitations are not acceptable, but understood. If ever a time should come when he forgets this, he is immediately reminded.

The black man has been psychologically contained through the use of negative reinforcement. Every time he steps over the line, he is punished. Eventually one decides to stride along side the line, but never cross it. He has been emotionally contained by the use of force by law enforcement agencies. He is not allowed to actively voice, or show his disapproval of his oppressors. If so, he is beaten down physically, and this is the last containment option. Still he is considered the strength, and being so, he is restrained, contained, and in some cases trained to accept his position.

Some of today's black men are reclaiming their psychological, emotional, and physical health. They are focusing their strength from inside of self. Their minds, hearts and souls are the treasure chests full of all the positive emotions that have not been allowed to surface. They are becoming strong within self in ways the oppressor cannot touch, or harm them. They know their women are where true strength abides for the women have nurtured them through the rough times. They have kept black men alive to arrive in this place at this time to deal with this modern day oppressor. They know their women for who they are and that they are their blessing.

Knowledge of self is being restored unto him, and he is listening. He is becoming....

(Black men and AIDS)

No one wants to hear; *"You have HIV, or Acquired Immune Deficiency Syndrome."* Many black men with HIV are becoming more responsible about taking care of themselves. The more they know about the disease, the more prone they are to take medications after the initial shock of finding out they have it. Their attitudes before acquiring the disease are typical of many men *and* women.

Many people refuse to use condoms regardless of the risk they face. They want nothing between them and their partners during sex. They also think they are immune to diseases rampant in society. If their partner is not a drug addict, and doesn't look diseased, they believe they have nothing to worry about. No matter how many times these opinions are proven wrong; they continue to put themselves at risk until HIV strikes home. Education about HIV and AIDS has been available to the general public for many years now. There is no excuse for ignorance regarding it.

Black men high on drugs do not know, nor care about news of HIV. Acquiring drugs is top priority with them. Black, male drug addicts using hypodermic needles are more at risk to themselves and the people they sleep with. Sharing needles increases that risk. No one really knows how many people have been infected this way. What is known is how they transmit it to others. One night stands, prostitutes, and spouses are likely candidates for infection.

Black youth are leading the way in lowering AIDS transmission by limiting their sex lives. Teenage pregnancy is down ten percent which indicates abstinence, or the use of condoms. Young black men are getting the message and choosing life over drugs and slow deterioration of their bodies by a disease that can be avoided.

What will the down-low brothers say to their wives and families? What happens when they find out you have acquired the disease?

This should be a wake up call for all black males still carelessly seeking conquests. The use of condoms is no longer an option. It is a necessity. Lifestyle changes are crucial.

(White men and AIDS)

The same situation regarding many black men with HIV, holds true for many white men as well. They are motivated by the same sexual drives, drug problems, and immoral behaviors. The only difference may be the wherewithal to obtain better medical treatments when infected with HIV. This could mean better control of the disease and longer life expectancy. Many of them lend themselves to medical research in hopes of cures. Otherwise, the progression of the disease renders them both equal even unto death. Race plays no favorites when this disease works its way through the body. White men are also guilty of ignoring information about HIV. It seems to be a *male thing* to feel invincible, and immune.

Wives and girlfriends find it most difficult to convince men to seek medical help when something is amiss. When men are infected with the AIDS virus, medical treatment is usually sought during the latter stages of the disease that is usually when a major sickness occurs.

Causes of infection stems from homosexual liaisons, blood transfusions, sharing of drug needles, prostitution, and contact with someone with HIV. In most of these contacts, the use of condoms is avoided. Again, the need to have close contact with sexual partners takes priority over safety.

Spouses and children are the innocent victims of HIV and AIDS. Transmission through semen infects wives and fetuses with the virus. Women with HIV can transmit it to their unborn babies. Some HIV infected babies die early on and others live for many years before they succumb. This is the greatest tragedy of all.

Bisexuality may be an enjoyable lifestyle for some of these men, but what about the consequences that it presents? Are you willing to accept those consequences?

Although broken down by black and white men, HIV knows no color line, nor does it respect any person. All case scenarios can happen in any race of people, and to men and women alike.

Superman is not real and Superwoman does not exist!

(Black women supported the Million-Man March)

Quiet as it is kept, most black women did support the Million-Man March. Some were so avid in their support that they couldn't stay away. The media tried the *divide and conquer* theme by airing names of women distancing themselves from the march... Those names will not be mentioned here to further assist them.

Some black women did not lend their support for the following reasons:

"Black women have always been on the front lines of the struggle." This is true. Black women have been responsible for most of the gains afforded Blacks since they were brought to America. This does not mean black men do not need to collectively take responsibility to do their part. This does not mean black women are considered outside the struggle. It only means black men are going to take a more active role in it.

"Why should black women stay home?" All of us should be there." Sometimes it is best to allow men to come together alone to accomplish something. The same applies to women. Sometimes it is best for everyone to come together to get things done. This time it was best for black men to come together in order to heal and concentrate on themselves. Only they can decide what role they will play in the renaissance-taking place within the black community.

Black women should have been proud to stay home to watch such an historic event. The beauty of over a million black men standing up for self and the survival of their people were stupendous.

"There are things black women need to atone for too." This may be true, but black women have been the *keepers of the flame* for their men and children. The Million-Man March was not the time to find that *one-in-a-million man*. If there had been a large number of women at the march, the men would not have focused on the purpose of being there. They would have been distracted to a great degree, and black women know that for a fact. Conversations among many black women during the march were about finding a man in D.C.

(White women took a neutral stance during the Million-Man March)

There was little response from white women regarding the Million-Man March. Female newscasters were *very* low-keyed. The few negative respondents were of no significance to the march. White women were more curious than anything else. They were not comfortable with Min. Louis Farrakhan as a whole, but they asked questions about him. They interviewed many high-profile Blacks, and did not make blanket judgments as their male counterparts often did. Their main concern seemed to have been what would happen in Washington, D.C. during the march, and what it meant to Blacks in the future. They seemed to be sifting for answers before the event in order to maintain some sense of order within their own frame of reference (white, middle-class).

Blacks must remember that most Whites cannot understand black motivation in doing such things like *marching on Washington*. Most Whites do not have to deal with hostility on a daily basis. They do not have to be in constant struggle in order to compete against almost impossible odds. They don't understand black rage, and why they are the cause of it. They are adrift in La La Land where everything is honky-dory, and they just don't want to hear any bad news, or deal with any unpleasant thing. They want to enjoy the American Dream without hearing about anyone's nightmares.

White women can, and should be the strongest supporters of black causes. Their destiny is entwined with that of all minorities. Although they hold the distinction of being white in a white-dominated society, they must know they also bear the responsibility of helping to create positive change for all peoples. They attached themselves to black causes when it was en vogue. They became comfortable in the gains they made in regard to Affirmative Action. As soon as it was going full speed ahead, it became the target of the far right and gradually waned. Now Affirmative Action is on life support.

Is it Affirmative Action that is needed now? If not, what? The game has changed. A class war is in play. The upper class is waging war against the working class. And if the corporate powers have anything to say about it, there will be no working class. The jobs will be gone and homelessness will be the norm. This is the new battlefront.

(Black women have "Attitude.")

Sisters don't just walk they strut. They glide and stride with hips swaying from side to side just knowing the brothers are cued in. They move their heads on their shoulders in seemingly impossible ways. They can jerk this way and that, slide their head around in such a way, it would appear they have no *neck bones*. ☺

When they laugh, their eyes gleam like sunbeams as if their spirits are gazing upon the world through them. Beautiful as they are in joy, they can become frightening when afire with rage. Sisters possess many qualities, but the most discernable is their *attitude*. They have that staunch resistance to anything threatening.

They move and operate with a demeanor that is confident, resilient, controlled, intimidating, loving, powerful, sweet, haughty, and nurturing. These qualities may appear in different sisters according to their personalities. Some are coy, timid, and kind, but don't let that fool you. Many a soul has mistaken kindness for weakness. They are strong, *because* they are sisters. Others may appear cold, calculating and could tackle the world alone, but even they know it is a shield to keep the cruel world at bay. It is their protective armor needed when fending for self in a world of racism, sexism and hostility.

Sisters have rhythm Mother Africa bequeathed them upon departure from her shores. It tempers their interactions, soothes and calms their souls, infuses them with an inner world of calm while in the midst of painful emotional storms. Their rhythm attracts lovers who bask in the warmth of it when *the ladies* decide to share. Sisters display it in their dance moves as they gyrate to syncopated grooves as if entranced.

Yes, sisters have attitude, but they also have much more. They have love for life, and with all the pain confronting them, they still feel and express love. When sister-to-sister communication breaks down, no matter what happens between them, they are still there for each other. Even with all that attitude, they still have peace, patience, joy, and love.

(White women are passive)

There are quite a few passive white women, but they are not more passive than any other group of women. Their demeanors *are* more relaxed than the demeanors of black women. They can afford to relax in a world designed for their comfort. They are the billboard ladies. They are the image of ultimate beauty marketed for all womanhood in the world to pattern themselves. They have been tasked with the burden of being placed above all women by their men. White men seem determined to have the world glorify their women. White men have done an admirable job in placing her before the world, but in doing so, she is doomed to a life of turmoil trying to live up to that image. She has become prey for all kinds of men, for various reasons.

Passive white women are not powerless. They use submissiveness to attain status and obtain the best money can buy. You know the old saying grandmothers used to describe this tactic, *"You catch more flies with honey than you do vinegar."* Many black women have been under the impression that black men are attracted to white women because of their passivity, when in reality they are attracted to white women because they are different. Black men have been around black women all of their lives.

Now opportunities have arisen for them to branch out without the threat of lynching, maiming, and death, so they are partaking to the point of saturation. It can become sickening to black women. It has definitely become annoying. It does little for the egos of black women to be rejected by men of their own race.

Although myths about both races of women are still widespread, once analyzed, it is clear that the only people profiting from the myths are men.

Passivity means to accept without resistance. All women have been guilty of it at one time or another. All women share human traits. Only cultural idiosyncrasies are unique in each group. This is not to say that all cultures create passive women, but some women in every culture may be passive. This is due to upbringing and personality.

(Black women and AIDS)

AIDS cases have grown among black women in the past few years. They are contracting it from spouses, boyfriends, blood transfusions, and infected needles.

Promiscuity by mates unwilling to share information about their own illness for fear of rejection has left many women ignorant of their exposure to this deadly disease. By the time they find out, it is too late for treatment that would have been instrumental in saving their lives, the lives of their children, and possibly that of their unborn babies. Sometimes men do not realize they have been infected until their wives become ill. Many have accused their wives of infidelity to mask their own guilt. This is the horror of promiscuity today. One night of pleasure has brought too much pain to the undeserving.

It is also true of men seeking conquests while in relationships. They run the risk of becoming HIV positive every time they have unprotected sex. Their girlfriends are unknowingly playing with fire. If these men cared about themselves, they would wear condoms. Protecting themselves and women from pregnancy should be their first priority. A disease as deadly as AIDS should inspire them to take precautions, but it has not gotten their collective attention.

Hospitals should be more responsible than they are when transfusing blood. Since they are not, it would behoove all of us to donate our own blood for our surgeries. This is not always possible. Whenever blood is to be given, both men and women should question if the blood has been tested. No one cares more about you, than you. After all, *you are the only you, you have!* Protect yourself.

Drug use is an unfortunate reality for an unknown number of black women. Many of them end up with HIV and AIDS. Some of them share needles with other addicts which is the highest risk factor. It is extremely difficult to help these women while they are on the street. Often pregnancy brings them to hospitals where the innocent are born to die.

(White women and AIDS)

White women are privy to the same causes of contracting HIV and AIDS as anyone else. *If you have unprotected sex, it's just a matter of time!* The number of HIV and AIDS victims is rising among white women also. Their men suffer from the same improprieties as black men, infecting them and their unborn children.

A married man was involved in relationships with a man and a girlfriend. His wife was unaware of his promiscuous behavior. Three people were sharing his affections and each of them assumed they were his only lovers. He contracted HIV from his male lover and passed it on to his girlfriend and wife. He was afraid to tell his wife that she might be HIV positive. He was content to continue having sex with her with the possibility of infecting her, than to face the embarrassment and shame of telling her about his affairs. He planned to love her to *death.*

White women must become educated about HIV and AIDS, learn how to avoid it, and demand monogamous behavior from their spouses. As seen above, marriage is no defense against it. Everyone, married or single, should get an HIV test. Trust of spouses is not the issue here, preservation of life is.

We hear of quite a bit of swinging going on in white marriages. That's not to say that other ethnic groups do not participate in this type of behavior, but Whites tend to flaunt it on television and in tabloids. They seem to glory in the fact that they are doing something outside of the norm that makes them special. This type of behavior is a welcoming mat for HIV.

There are no innocent bystanders when it comes to unprotected sex. Everyone is responsible for themselves in today's sexual playground. If you play without your raincoat in the rain, you will get wet. *If you have sex without protection, you are privy to diseases.*

No one is quite sure how many people in America are infected with the AIDS virus, but we do know numbers are rising. Statistics show that one person comes into contact with the disease every minute of every day in this country. What does it take to wake everyone up?

(Black women want black men with money)

All women want men with money. Reality sets in when women mature, and they begin to look for men with potential to *make money*. Black women are not unique in wanting to mate with someone with financial stability. They have seen their grandmothers and mothers sacrificing year end and year out. They want a better life.

Young girls and young women today are vocally expressive about what they want in a man. They are particular about the type of car a young man drives, and whether his clothes are top of the line. He must have a j-o-b, and if he takes her out to dinner, McDonalds is definitely not on the menu.

Young men today are pressured to provide for their ladies beyond their ability to produce. Unemployment rates are in the double digits for black youth and black men. They are the least likely candidates for employment in high scale jobs.

College educated black men are finding it almost impossible to find employment. When they do, it is usually at a pay scale below that of white youth with the same credentials. This unfair situation leaves many black men without the financial resources to satisfy the appetites of young black women. Some of the uneducated have chosen criminal lifestyles as a way to accumulate cash to appease the women they want to impress. Many women in their thirties, forties, *and* fifties are also less inclined to date men without the finances to *adequately* woo them. They are mature enough to know that money doesn't make the man, but they too are expressing, *"Ain't nothin' goin' on, but the rent." "No romance without finance." "You gotta have a j-o-b, if you want to be with me."*

Average every day sisters are not money hungry. They will settle for men willing to work with them to build lives together. They are realistic and understand the plight of black men in this country. These are the women men are looking for, and usually end up with after having gone through experiences dating women with unrealistic expectations.

(White women want love from black men)

White women want love like other women. That is not the only reason they are attracted to, and fall in love with black men. They want no more from black men than black women. They also want someone to respect, and take care of them. They tend to put up with more *from* black men than black women do, however.

In every large black neighborhood in America, there are a sprinkle of white women paired with black male boyfriends, or spouses. In many cases they have sacrificed their families and friends to be with the man they have chosen, or who has chosen them. Blacks within these communities become friends and associates of these couples, and are aware of their relationships, especially the women. They talk about their relationships with each other and more often than not, black women have found that white women are more apt to allow the men full control of the relationship. They do what they are told in many cases.

The obvious human reaction, after a long period of adjustment to an alien situation, is to either become rebellious demanding independence, or accepting fate as it is and remaining submissive. Many white women have chosen the former. The mysteries of the relationships have worn off. They know whom they are dealing with, and refuse to any longer accept mistreatment, abuse, irresponsibility, neglect, and being treated like a possession rather than an individual. This is not to say all black men treat white women this way, but the few who have, are beginning to understand how unhappy these women really are.

The men know black women would not accept such behaviors from them, so they choose women they think they can control, and will not make them accountable for their actions and inactions. Time has placed them into a precarious situation. These women *are* rebelling. No longer is there a group of women they can take advantage of because of their so-called *black mystique*. They must now tow the line.

Conclusion

There have been an indeterminate number of relationships between black and white men and women. They have ranged from the vilest to the most revered. These relationships did not begin with European colonialism of the African continent. It began in ancient times long before there was an institution of *racism*.

When Africans ruled the world; such as it was at the time, there *was* no Europe. People of fair complexions were scattered, poor, and looked to the Africans for sustenance. Their envy of African wealth and educational superiority reached a climax when they discovered gunpowder in China. With this lethal force, along with the beginning of physical and psychological control of the masses, they began the gradual extermination of the people they perceived as the greatest threat, the Africans.

The first and foremost restriction of Africans once the slave trade was instituted was the knowledge of self and history. This has enabled Whites to excel using the creative talents of Blacks without having to give credit.

This symbiotic relationship holds true today in daily interactions. Conscious knowledge of what is actually going on between black men and women with white men and women is ever present in the minds of Blacks. They make the choice to play the subservient role, or empower themselves to be true to self by looking each man or woman in the eye demanding respect and equality in treatment.

Only Whites know what *they* are thinking. Are they consciously treating black people different than others? They will have to solve their own dilemmas of race. Blacks can only make them aware of the overt and covert inequities.

No matter what tactics they use to bridge the historic, cultural and racial divide, Blacks and Whites must conclude at some point that the gender attractions will never go away. Men love women. Women love men. Differences in race have proven to be more of an attraction than a deterrent in these relationships. We're all guilty of being human. We love.

Chapter Five

Politics, Etc.

(Blacks were not surprised by Texaco executive's racist remarks)

"This diversity thing, you know how black jelly beans agree." Response: *"That's funny. All the black jelly beans seem to be glued to the bottom of the bag." "I'm still having trouble with Hanukkah. Now, we have Kwanzaa...-- niggers, they--all over us with this."*

The place where fear of Blacks is nonexistent is in the boardrooms and meeting rooms throughout corporate America. The Texaco incident was not a unique situation. It is common practice for Whites in high positions behind closed doors to vilify other groups. They are in their safety zones with like-minded people and feel free to speak at will. So happens, an individual who knew his days were numbered in the organization, taped the proceedings to give the world a sneak preview of what actually goes on when the world is believed to be out of earshot.

It makes one wonder what is being said behind closed doors today in companies where Whites still feel secure in their convictions that Blacks will never be allowed upward mobility. Each of them should be researched for their record in hiring and promotion of minorities. It would be wonderful if more people would come forward because it is the right thing to do rather than as an act of revenge.

The above revelations are no surprise to Blacks. Whites are stunned, but the black community has endured worse. This has been part of the price Blacks have had to pay for inclusion into a society that is not comfortable with them. Blacks sense the resentment, but are compelled to endure it in order to remain employed.

When minorities are treated adversely by middle management, there is a clear indication that racism exists at the top. Middle managers must feel comfortable in their actions and treatment of Blacks. This comfort probably stems from knowing the attitudes at the top. This is a widespread problem that is a testimonial for the need for Affirmative Action.

Changing people's attitude is a horse of a different color. This takes place in homes, schools, and communities. The prevalent attitudes in them groom people like the ones above.

(Whites were amazed by remarks made by Texaco executives)

News reports in all media showed the shocking effects the Texaco story had on Whites across the country. Many thought it unbelievable, some expressed sadness that this was still going on, and still others shrugged as if to say, *"So what?"*

The news media focused on those stunned by the news. This reaction seems rather jaded. Do most Whites really believe they are better qualified than Blacks who have not been allowed to move up within *their* organizations? They know there are inequities within the business world. They hover together during lunch, and talk to each other off-hours discussing why, *"That Nigger better not get that position. I worked hard for it, and I am the one deserving of it."* They *know* how prevalent racism is because they practice it. Blacks working with them also *know* how Whites benefit from racist practices within organizations. The feigning of surprise and shock is a slap in the face to Blacks.

Most Whites were probably annoyed that the Texaco execs were not more discreet in their evaluation of black employees. In other words, *"It's O.K. to discriminate. Just don't let the world know that you're doing it."* The aftermath of views clearly supports this attitude.

Radio talk shows were overwhelmed with calls from Whites in disagreement with the boycott against Texaco. Many of them felt private business should be able to do whatever it wants in regard to its employees' advancement. Philadelphia WWDB callers were so vocally abusive to Blacks that this author had to call in to chastise them for exhibiting blatant racism. One went so far as to say a race war was quickly approaching. Is that what they subconsciously fear, or is it a conscious desire?

It would be interesting to discover how many Whites are truly amazed, and how many are sympathetic to minority struggles for equality. We already know there are multitudes benefiting from the suffering of others. Could they be the silent majority watching from the sidelines?

(Blacks find it easy to believe reports regarding possible CIA involvement in trafficking drugs into the black community)

The U.S. Government finally admitted it was responsible for the Tuskegee Syphilis experimentation on black men after over twenty years of denial. Proof of government involvement was made public forcing a high level official to come forward.

A large group of black men (over 100) were injected with syphilis, allowed to continue their normal lives while doctors observed over many years the progressive effects of the disease on their bodies. They were used as human guinea pigs. The impact the disease had on the black community wasn't considered.

During the 1960s, governmental agencies (CIA-FBI) infiltrated black organizations with the prime objective being to render them ineffective. They succeeded.

The CIA has been accused of flooding black communities with drugs in the 1980s. Two white men and one black have come forward to accuse the agency. There are supposedly documents proving CIA involvement. No proof has been released to the public at the time of this writing. The Congressional Black Caucus and the CIA did investigations. The CIA investigating itself has been questioned, but to no avail.

None of the above fosters good will within black communities. Disbelief of governmental agencies has been fueled by their continuous deceit. They send their slickest smooth talking representatives forward to defend them. They smile slyly, sidestep questions, and most likely continue to cover up wrong doing against citizens.

There can never be trust in the government as long as it treats Blacks as a dispensable commodity to be used, abused, and misused. This has historically been the case and remains so today. Will this notorious behavior be allowed to further devastate people of color?

(Whites feign disbelief of possible CIA heinous behavior)

Actually, quite a few Whites do not want to believe the CIA would be used against Blacks as a racial group. They are more prone to believe the agency goes after spies and people trying to overthrow the government. The idea that the agency could possibly flood drugs into any neighborhood is so far removed form everything they know and believe. The majority of Whites were reared in an America where there was no fear of police, or any agency created for the defense of their country. It is difficult for them to believe that there are groups of people in this country experiencing the wrath and clandestine eavesdropping of these agencies every day because of the color of their skin.

It is also common belief among many Blacks that dossiers being kept on them, especially if they were at all involved in the Civil Rights movement in the 1960s and beyond.

Whites see this as paranoia on the part of Blacks, but paranoia is a defense mechanism for self-preservation. When you are unwelcome, unwanted, experimented on, abused, and treated unfairly, would paranoia be considered an unreasonable reaction? Reasonable minds would think not.

The possibility that some Whites will demand the truth be told now instead of a twenty year wait like the Tuskegee admission is a relief to Blacks that maybe now some of them are waking up to the reality of life in America. If not, when the agencies become invincible in time, white skin will not be invulnerable to infiltration into the lives of Americans now free of such tactics.

Whites aware of what is going on within the above agencies, remain quiet either out of fear for themselves, or dislike for the victims. Are these people without a conscience, or hard core racists? Are they programmed into automatons for governmental use? Are the agencies so diabolical that anything they do is acceptable? Are they so entrenched and powerful that no one is willing to challenge them out of fear?

(Black leaders emerge from the group)

There are no black leaders in the black community. White people call them *black leaders,* but black people do not. There are people who emerge from the group to speak on behalf of the group. They are not afraid to speak out against injustice. Some have political affiliation, some religious, some organizational, and some, none at all.

Examples of these kinds of people are; Jesse Jackson, Louis Farrakhan, Martin Luther King, Jr., Malcolm X, Fannie Lou Hamer, Paul Robeson, Marcus Garvey, and W.E.B. Du Bois. Two have been assassinated, and have been maligned and jailed. Some have seen their careers flushed away, and others still survive because they play the game by white rules, or they have protection Whites fear. Whites consider them all black leaders.

Black people as a whole admire those who *step to* adversaries of Blacks, but they do not consider them leaders. Webster defines leader as; *"a person who has commanding authority or influence."* There is no one today having commanding authority over all black people. They may influence some black people, but the numbers cannot be determined to assume they lead all black people, or that all black people think and support their points of view.

All Blacks are leaders in today's battle for equality and justice. If a so-called leader is struck down, they will continue to rise, one by one until equality and justice become a reality for people of color in America and the world. Black people do not need leaders they need results.

Blacks do not have to be on one accord philosophically in order to obtain justice in America. They need to stand up for what is right, and encourage their white, brown, yellow, and red friends to do the same.

When we all stand together demanding true justice for all, that will be the day we all embrace the American dream. All people within our borders will know the spirits, minds, and hearts of us all. When that happens this will truly be the United States of America.

(Whites choose acceptable black leaders)

The press often starts calling high-profile Blacks, leaders. Christian ministers are the most acceptable white choices for black leadership. Rev. Al Sharpton and Rev. Jesse Jackson are just two ministers given continued press coverage catapulting them onto the national scene. Once there, it is difficult for the individuals to back down from their positions. They feel compelled to lead. We all know the old adage, *leadership was thrust upon me*. These types of ministers believe in Christianity as taught in Judeo-Christian doctrines. Not the *eye-for-an-eye* part, but rather the nonviolent *love thy neighbor as thyself* part. The part that supports, *don't go out there killing white folks*. They are acceptable enough to Whites because they signify everything good about the humanity of man, while Whites are performing everything bad in regard to inhumanity to mankind. As long as the killing is done by them, it is considered fighting for *the interests of the country,* but no one is suppose to fight against their injustice. Their warning is *retaliation with a vengeance.*

Some ministers are not acceptable to Whites. Especially those greeting with the words, *As-Salaam Alaikem!* Min. Louis Farrakhan is considered a threat, and is not supported by Whites. His belief in self-protection and striking back at an enemy is totally unacceptable. The mere thought of Blacks physically retaliating against Whites is their greatest fear. The truth he speaks, angers, exposes, and ridicules them in front of the world.

The slant they give him in the press is designed to program Whites *and Blacks* against him. They often misquote him, and send pro-racist black reporters to spy on him. His clout in the black community had grown because of their efforts to discredit him.

Min. Al Sharpton is also unacceptable to whites. He's a so-called *troublemaker* because he also exposes their ugly side to the world. They *can live without this, thank you.* When there is an inequity of justice, he shows up to spotlight it.

(Blacks support Min. Louis Farrakhan)

Not all Blacks support Min. Louis Farrakhan. It would not be surprising if surveys indicated most Blacks appreciate him stepping out on the national scene. Without him, another view of the struggle for justice and equality would be lost to them. His hard hitting, no-holds-barred rhetoric is needed for those not open to various other voices out there.

There are poor as well as educated Blacks who are tired of the run-of-the-mill, *we shall overcome* record. They are ready to actively participate in doing something tangible. They want guidance on how they can play a part in changing things. There is a silent majority in support of Min. Farrakhan.

The Million-Man March afforded over a million black men an opportunity to do just that. No other so-called leader called on black men to take responsibility for themselves and their people. Min. Louis Farrakhan did. He, along with others, also devised a plan extending many years into the future for the economic betterment of black people.

Black people come out in great numbers to hear him speak throughout the country. They give money to support causes he asks them to support. He has a great deal of influence in the black community because he is visible and caring.

Black people do not consider Min. Farrakhan to be their leader. He is a man vocal in the support of racial pride, and critical of racial injustice. In fact, many black people consider him a trouble maker. They think he causes white people to further dislike Blacks, and they agree with Whites in labeling him a hate monger. They miss the main idea.

Black people do not need white people to like them. They need Whites to respect them, and their rights. His statements about Whites should be examined, and if they are true statements, he should be respected for having the courage to speak out.

Whites should not underestimate his following. He is our brother.

(Whites are afraid of Min. Louis Farrakhan)

Many Whites would totally disagree with this statement. Since nothing is absolute, it would be safe to say some Whites are afraid of the power Min. Farrakhan may have. They do not fear him personally, but politically, he may be a very real threat. Some Whites have been heard to say they feel he could stir up Blacks to kill Whites. This nonsense is just that, nonsense.

Blacks do not have an innate urge to kill white people. Blacks want equality and equal access to all the things Whites already have. That *is* the bottom line for Blacks. They don't want to take anything away from anyone else. They want the same rules to apply to *everyone,* and some want back payment for work already performed. That, by any sane person's logic, is a reasonable request.

The media has tarnished and shaped Min. Farrakhan's image to the point where Whites can hardly distinguish the image from the man. The Million-Man March did more to show the *real man.* Whites were asking Blacks all over America, *"Where is the Louis Farrakhan I've been reading about. The man I saw on television didn't seem to be all that bad? He didn't say anything repulsive or mean spirited. I really liked what he had to say."* Some Whites have changed their view of him. They realized their fear was unfounded. That is, until they saw the news.

The slanted broadcast on the evening of the Million-Man March, was an obvious attempt to mislead people to believe that the person they saw was not the real Louis Farrakhan. They wanted Whites to believe he was putting on a show for them. This didn't work for most, because he was directing his speech to black people. His demeanor, sincerity, religious conviction, and articulation could not be faked as far as they were concerned.

The efforts by those in control of the media could not erase what people saw with their own eyes and felt with their hearts. Although many still have reservations, they now understand a little better who this man is. In fact, some Whites liked him.

(Blacks supported the Million-Man March)

It can be said without reservation that most Blacks did support the Million-Man March and the Million-More Movement on Washington. Some Blacks, who did not support the marches because of Min. Louis Farrakhan and Rev. Benjamin Chavis' part in it, have rethought their positions. Overwhelming support came from the *Black community* that nullifies any other so-called leader's efforts to play down the significance of the march.

Many so-called black leaders did not want to raise the ire of white benefactors, friends, and supporters of their organizations. They also did not want to be considered *one of those kinds of Negroes.* They want to be generals in the war on racism, but would rather distance themselves from the fields of battle. If they consider themselves to be champions fighting for the rights of their people, they must be willing to *step to* those causing the terrible plight of their people. This means they should stand tall in unity when a righteous, self propelled, self determination call is made that is beneficial to *the people* and not just to, and for themselves.

The masses of Blacks and other minorities understood. They could *feel it.* Something was in the air. The closer the date of the events, the stronger the *vibes* became to unite as one. The marches were about unity and becoming whole again. They were about breaking the chains of slave mentality. They were about breaking away from doing what others wanted Blacks to do, to doing what Blacks must do for the benefit and survival of all.

The Million-Man March was not about women standing up, and being counted along with men. It was about men standing up for *themselves,* taking ownership for *their* own misdeeds, repenting for *their* own sins, taking responsibility for *own* lives, and making pledges to change *their* behavior.

Black women have longed for the day when black men would stand up and be counted. Now that they have, what are black women afraid of? It is time for black men to reclaim the reins of the struggle.

(Whites denounced the Million-Man March)

Wherever one looked, whether it was in the newspapers, magazines, or on television, there was the face of Min. Louis Farrakhan depicted as a racist, troublemaker, and Jew hater. Since that is the image Whites were most likely to encounter, it gave them the impression that this was the true essence of the man.

When word of the Million-Man March hit the news full force; many efforts were made by white newscasters bombarding the media showing Min. Louis Farrakhan in the worst possible light to negate the importance of the march. Many Whites agreed with the image of him, and coupled it with information previously programmed into them through the years.

Whites did not support the march and its leaders, although some of them liked the *reasons* for it. The fact that Blacks were going to Washington and did not ask for anything, made them sigh with relief. The fact that one million black men were going to Washington frightened many of them. They didn't expect peace, calm and a day filled with cooperation, brotherhood, and love. They expected many incidents involving the police. When this did not happen, many Whites saw, for the first time, a large number of black men together without trouble. They knew the stereotypical image of black men, but on that day they saw black men in reality.

The march did for the image of black men what media had taken over a hundred years to destroy. For once, the media was forced to show the truth in spite of itself. Of course, it came back the eve of, and the next day to tell people they didn't really see *that* many black men together in one place, but since you can't fool all the people all the time, people believed what they saw with their own eyes.

The white community *was abuzz* with, *"Nothing is going to come of it. Wait to see what happens when they go home. I predict absolutely nothing."* Well, white America, something is happening. The black community *is abuzz* because **a new brother is in town.**

(Blacks see themselves as Americans)

This statement is true in some cases. One would think anyone born in America would consider themselves American. Some black people do not consider themselves true Americans because they do not reap the benefits accorded that status. One of the benefits is being treated equally under the law. This is indeed a valid observation. Another is being given equal access to jobs and housing. This too is valid along with many other reasons they give for separating themselves from the term.

The majority of Blacks, however, do consider themselves Americans. They were born and reared in America. They support her when she is good, and chastise her when she is bad. They feel they have stock in her, and demand she deliver what she promises to all her citizens. They pay taxes into her collective coffers, participate in the economy, attend her schools, sit on her juries, vote in her elections, fight in her wars, and seal their fate with hers. They do all the things required of all citizens.

When the President speaks for Americans, he speaks for them. When the economy is not doing well, they feel the pinch like everyone else. When there is a national disaster, they contribute money, aid and roll up their sleeves to assist. When Americans are called on for anything, Blacks are there to answer the call.

No one need question where the hearts of black Americans are. The black struggle *in* America has been for more inclusiveness. The struggle today continues for the same reason. Laws exist for this purpose, but convincing white Americans has been disheartening at best.

Blacks have paid the highest price for the longest time. They have been the ones treated the worse, for no reason at all. They have been the most loyal, faithful, and long suffering of all citizens. They have contributed the most, for the least reward. Yes, Blacks are true Americans next in line behind Native Americans. Everyone else, fall in behind *them*.

(Whites see Blacks as "the Black Community," but not as Americans)

Some Whites do believe Blacks are not true Americans. They give themselves away when they speak on certain issues. On a recent radio talk show, a white lady called in concerning President Clinton's statement regarding the murder of Israeli Prime Minister Yitzhak Rabin. The President used the term *Americans* to extend the nation's condolences to all the Israeli people.

Her question was "Why hasn't anyone from the black community spoken out on this. *They are quick to speak out on everything else, but not one has spoken out on this issue.*" She completely separated black Americans from the *Americans* President Clinton was speaking on behalf of. That separation indicated her point of view regarding black Americans.

It can be concluded that she does not see Blacks as inclusive with all other Americans. *They* are *the Black community.* Let this resound loud as the rolling sea. **When black Americans deal with America, we *are* the "Black Community." When an American President speaks to the world, he is speaking for *all* Americans and that includes the "Black Community."**

Now that that issue is cleared up we can proceed. The lady above is indicative of many Whites who see Blacks the same way. Because of the unique position of Blacks in America, Whites really don't know how to deal *with* Blacks. They don't know what to say, how to say it, or even if they should say it. Under these circumstances, the best thing to do is ask a simple question. If one is not sure of what to do, either don't do it, or ask a question concerning it. This way both parties are comfortable with the situation, and the conversation.

Blacks are the part of America that reminds America of who she is, and what she stands for. Whenever Whites forget it, they can be assured blacks will be there. When Blacks are there, the rights of all the people are safeguarded. Thank GOD *for* the "Black Community."

(Black support of Civil Rights opens doors for all minorities)

Without the Civil Rights struggle throughout the years, many women and all minority ethnic groups within this country would not realize the growth and upward mobility now existent in American society. Every opportunity to participate in industry, be it on an occupational level, or minority business set-asides, was probably provided by black people struggling for inclusiveness for all people.

Isn't it ironic that the people who struggled so diligently for desegregation have not reaped the rewards as have other ethnic groups who were impassioned observers during the many marches, freedom rides, confrontations with police, and a multitude of battering and death knells?

White women, Hispanics, and Asians have become the *chosen ones*. They are considered less threatening, and they satisfy quotas and goals set by federal guidelines. This loophole adds salt to the wounds of a people still exposed to America's misplaced hatred of them.

When a war is fought and won, one does not expect an outside force to reap the benefits of one's struggles. The spoils are supposed to go to the victor. In the case of the civil rights struggle in this country, the powers that be have, yet again, eased their way out of taking responsibility for past injustices.

Since white women are considered minority, the powerbrokers have given their wives, sisters, and daughters the bulk of the spoils. A few crumbs have been allocated to Blacks to quell the anger. Today's legislative bodies are working around the clock to sweep those crumbs away by *downsizing* on state and federal levels. Many companies are rebuilding on foreign soil, or in rural white populated areas of the country.

All of the pain, struggle, lynching, and sacrifice of a people castrated by slavery, and bound by white supremacy have benefited little. What manner of man denies GOD's people their birthright?

(White rejection of inclusion is growing)

As America becomes more conservative, the purse strings are drawing tighter. White Americans are growing weary of *the black situation*.

The death knells for Affirmative Action rang loud and clear in California in 1996. This was just the beginning. White America paused with bated breath awaiting a signal for the rest of the country. Although the challenge is on in the courts, many states are proposing to do the same.

Layoffs from the largest Fortune 500 companies have left many whites without employment. High salary levels have dropped significantly causing them to compete for jobs at a lower level. This means they have to compete with minority persons for jobs Whites were reluctant to pursue in the past. They feel they should be considered first and foremost simply because *they* think they are more qualified, and they definitely have the inside track *because* they are white.

Whites benefit from discriminatory practices in companies, but many will not admit it. There are some who believe in inclusion because they believe in fairness and can hold their own no matter what the competition. Many others know how privileged they are, and to their way of thinking embracing Affirmative Action would mean economical suicide. They know they have reached their *Peter Principle* within the organization. Evidence of this can be seen in just about every occupation in America. Texaco is not unique.

Corporate level discrimination is a given, as most Blacks already know. It is the federal and state job levels of discrimination that is highly hypocritical. These institutions laud themselves for non-discriminatory practices claiming civil service exams determine hiring and promotional opportunities. When actual hiring and promotions take place, white managers using the *law of three* have three people to choose from, and most often it is someone white.

(Black trust has delayed progress)

Putting total faith in people unconcerned with you or your welfare is not wise. It leaves you and yours in a very precarious position. Nothing you do or say will motivate them to help you. They are motivated by their needs, not yours. If it suits them for you to remain where you are, no amount of cajoling will help. They must be given the thing most precious to them. If you are aware of what that one *thing* is, and produce it, you can motivate them to move mountains out of your way.

There must be a return for most Whites for them to put themselves on the line for anyone, including each other. Concern is for self first and foremost. All others pay cash.

This has been the relationship between Blacks and Whites in America since the abolition of slavery. Blacks have been waiting for folks to *come to their senses*. Because of patience on the part of Blacks, progress has been sluggish at best. The misconception has been that white people have thinking patterns like people of color. There has never been a greater fallacy.

Seeking group equality within a society known for rewarding individual accomplishment is a tough proposition. Rewards given any group legally, morally, or for humane considerations are usually secured through intimidation, extreme unrelenting pressure, or civil upheaval. All tactics mentioned have been utilized in the struggle for civil rights.

Economic pressure is the one *thing* most effective in creating change in today's society. If applied correctly, Atlas will shrug. If Blacks used boycott methods mentioned earlier, they would accomplish goals quicker. Businesses in America know what the future holds. They know projections made by demographers concerning future consumer markets. They also know people of color will be their largest consumer group.

(White manipulation of trust has furthered their objectives)

Unfortunately, this statement is true. Manipulation of the masses maintains control over them. Blacks are not exempt from this psychological technique. In fact, they are exclusively manipulated by the use of appeasement and delay tactics. Whenever the wheel squeaks too loudly, it is oiled to keep it quiet, out of sight and out of mind.

This trial-by-error approach has gone wanting. Although laws are on the books to grant all people opportunity in America, tools used to program the masses are still feeding them outdated information. More aptly put, the forces in control are programming minds of the masses data they want them to believe. Evidence of this can be found in media output.

Wherever the media moguls want to mentally take the masses, the masses willingly follow. Media tells them which products to drink, wear, eat, purchase, and which personalities to adore. *Who is in this year, and who is out. He is the sexiest man alive. She is the most beautiful woman in the world. What is hot and what is not. The hottest videos you can rent and buy. The best cities in America families are choosing to move to. The hottest vacation spots to visit.* If you think you aren't being *handled,* think again.

Control of resources is also taking place. As long as the media can control a large area of our lives, they control where we spend our money. Children learn about hot toys from television. Their parents often purchase them. Adults *must* have that new computer system they saw advertised. What else is being manipulated?

Hidden racism can manipulate the masses deceitfully. *"We can grab black dollars without hiring **them**. Do not give them what they want; instead, give them what we think they should have. No sense in oiling the wheel again until we have to, hopefully we can hold them off a while longer. If we get rid of Affirmative Action, it should keep them busy for a while, don't you think?"*

(Black survival depends on black unity)

In a country with over 300 million people, 40 million Blacks is not a large number. They are approximately twelve percent of the population. If all Blacks unite to achieve a goal there is a chance they will succeed. If they do not, there is no chance at all.

Views of Blacks vary as much as do those of Whites. Blacks, however, cannot afford the luxury of infighting. All disagreements must be put aside for survival of the group. Be they Republican, Democrat, Catholic, Baptist, Fundamentalist, male, female, elite, poor, middle-class, entertainer, doctor, lawyer, aerospace engineer, athlete, movie star, or Supreme Court Justice, all people within the group *must* realize the importance of collective unity in pursuit of equality and justice in the United States of America.

None need like each other, nor agree politically. They must work, each in his or her choosing to diligently move forward the cause for all people to receive equal treatment and equal access to goods, services and employment. If they falter, and the house of cards collapses, those at the top have the most to lose. It would behoove all people of color to stand up for others as they do for themselves.

Too many Blacks are backbiting, and gossiping about those trying to make change. Rather than displaying obvious jealously, why not offer assistance? The rewards are immeasurable.

The Willie Lynch mentality era is drawing to a close. No longer are Blacks in the know going to let people get away with outmoded divisive behaviors. People are being read the riot act every day. *"If you are not part of the solution, you are part of the problem."* when a ship is sinking, everyone aboard is needed to bale water to keep it afloat. If part of the crew is asleep, some of them lazy, and yet a few others talking about the ones struggling to save the ship, the vessel and the entire crew is doomed. But if all pull together, they will survive.

(White survival depends on economic trends)

White survival is dependent on economics. As long as money is perceived as power, money, and those who controls it will rule and maintain power. Right now, Whites are in control of money markets around the world. That is why the President of the United States is considered the "King of the World." He is the President of the richest nation on earth. This means the country can buy and sell whatever it wishes whenever it wants, *and* to whomever it wants. This also means total control over people. That is, until the economy collapsed.

If a war needs to be fought, it will decide with whom and where it will happen. If this decision is taken away by *rebels*, it will squash them immediately if possible, gradually if necessary.

When the stock market is riding high, excitement fills the air. Money is being made. Actually it is changing hands. They like the game of transferring funds from one to another. Sometimes trickery is used, but mainly a battle of wits. There is a motivation factor involved in this game. The motivation is *accumulation*. The more one accumulates, the more successful one is. The tactics used are not important. If tactics used are not admirable ones, just don't get caught. If they are admirable, don't forget, *nice guys finish last*. Take the money and run.

When the stock market falls drastically or crashes mayhem is introduced into the equation. Murder-suicides performed by men left financially ruined are commonplace at such times. They kill their families and themselves when the prospect of poverty becomes clear. Disgrace before peers is another undesirable position. Death is sweeter than anticipation of a life less than that pursued and attained.

The main incentive to achieve wealth extends beyond the games. It derives from distancing oneself from poverty. The further away one gets the more rewards one receives. Grabbing the brass ring is the ultimate goal. How sad it must be to live an existence based on superficiality.

(Blacks as a whole do not support black Republicans)

This seems to be a true statement if polls and election results are any indication. Usually black Republicans are voted into office by majority white votes. Black Republicans quote the *party line* of the Republican Party that has alienated minorities throughout the country.

Black Republicans are a growing breed. They have attached themselves to a philosophy that there should be less governmental control, and people should do more for themselves without governmental assistance. This school of thought is not lost on Blacks and minorities. Most people in America agree with the above views. Republicans often take the stance that change should be immediate with little regard concerning the human factor.

Someone once said, "*Some people are Republicans because they can afford to be. I am a Democrat because I have to be.*" Democrats are *more* concerned with the *little guy*. Republicans seem to treat the average person with disdain. Their effort to railroad bills through Congress during the first six years of George W. Bush's administration was a clear example why Americans chose not to give them full reign in the 2009 elections.

All polls determined that Americans as a whole did not trust George W. Bush during his later reign. George W. made it into office with a very clear agenda. He achieved his goal, but devastated the country. Everyone will be reeling from his effects for many years to come.

Black Republicans are probably needed to balance the scale in both parties. The battle for justice must be fought on all sides. Black presence in the Republican Party is a necessary evil. They are not focused on the overall goal in the struggle for civil rights. If they are there as token pawns utilized by the party to garner black votes and to convince people that they are a party of inclusiveness, they have failed. Their presence serves only them and their controllers. They are *Uncle Tomming* their way up the political ladder.

(White Republicans overwhelmingly support black Republicans)

Most white Republicans are accepting of, but do not really want to rub shoulders with black Republicans. Their party has been one of non-inclusiveness and many of them like it that way.

The word speak they use key into race division. *We* mean white. *They* mean everyone else. *Our* is their pronoun for *white people*. When majority people classify others as *welfare recipients,* they invariably are talking about minorities, specifically Blacks. When they speak of *criminals,* they are talking about black men and black youth. The country as a whole knows this. Where have black Republicans been for the past thirty years? Are they only reading the message and not between the lines?

White Republicans have had to be prepared for the recruitment of black Republicans into the party. For the past twenty years, Republican politicians have been promoting the idea of bringing them aboard to create a broader constituent base. They have used radio talk shows and television programs to do that. It was more successful among the black elite than average working people because advantages offered were more suited to the upper class.

Anyone possessing significant amounts of money with the prospect of obtaining more, or approached with an option of paying lower taxes on the money they have are surely prone to listen to a platform that supports that agenda. People at the lower rungs of the financial strata are less prone to adhere to such a platform. They know someone has to pay those taxes, and if the rich doesn't the poor guy ends up paying the tab.

Whatever assistance Republicans can muster for their cause, they will welcome into the party. Money and influence supersedes race. If Blacks or a group unlike themselves can assist them in reaching their goals, white Republicans will use them for the time being. What happens after their ends have been achieved? Buckle your seat belts, guys!

(Blacks did not support President George W. Bush and his policies)

Not all Blacks supported President Bush as could be seen in earlier statements regarding Black Republicans. Those who do should not be taken for granted. Votes can easily shift to another party.

The lesser of two evils is the phenomenon taking place in America today. There is no perfect person with a perfect plan. There are only politicians taking the pulse of the American people in hopes of discerning which direction to take, and finding a solution to the quagmire of economic ups and downs, and problems plaguing us today.

No one knew what President Bush was going to do, but his attack on Iraq has plunged the country into an economic and moral depressed state. The new deficit has America bogged down in debt. Voters in all ethnic groups do not have to be rocket scientists to understand simple math. **You don't spend or bail out banks when there's nothing to give, stupid!** President Bush's plans were methodically put into action for six years by the republican congress. Implementation of the Patriot Act expanded his powers beyond that of any president in the past. Advancement for Blacks and all peoples within the country was stunted. Chopping off the head and expecting the body to follow is not conducive to a healthy economy that is the essence of the Republican plan.

Today, all of the advances during Clinton's terms have been amBUSHed. Many Americans are now left behind. George W's "Leave No Child Behind" has done just the opposite for America's children and citizenry. Corporations now own America, and all of its resources.

Blacks are still politically astute in spite of this setback. Their political sophistication far exceeds what politicians are led to believe. Lethargy at the polls in past years was a sign of hopelessness. Americans are becoming increasingly bold. Blacks are voting in larger numbers as is the rest of the nation. **Everyone needs an inoculation of hope. Let's continuously vote to change this trend!**

(Whites supported President George W. Bush and his policies)

The 2000 and 2004 presidential elections clearly proved that most Whites supported President Bush and his policies. Election fraud, now known as a given, did have an impact, but Whites believed him and his rhetoric and they *are* the majority in this country. They voted against their own best interests, and got what they voted for.

The mood of the nation was one of fear and the need to get their pound of flesh for the 9/11 attack. Before 2000, no one knew the hammer would fall on us all. Bush was that hammer that would send the economy and the world into a tailspin.

Diversity took a back seat. Whites had been on their way to gradually accepting inclusiveness. The adjustment to an America that was totally different than the one they were used to, would have been difficult, but the atmosphere was one of change. They should be commended for their progress during that time.

Decent people do not want harm to come to anyone. Many Whites are decent people. Many Whites do not want harm to come to anyone. We can conclude from this, that many Whites were ready for everyone to succeed. But 9/11 changed that course. They thought the only alternative left for them was to vote the straight Republican ticket next time to secure their futures without regard for anyone less fortunate. ***That is exactly what happened in 2000, and 2004 with help from the Supreme Court!*** Since then, the future of America hung in the balance.

President Clinton's policies remained successful as long as the voting populace saw value in them. If there was an economic plunge during his term (which there wasn't), their support would have shifted towards the Republican congress for relief. Whites willing to do what was fair for collective America were President Clinton's saving grace. In 2008 they were pondering which course to take. They experienced mean spirited, greedy forces in control in the Bush administration. Did they choose the right man this time? Electing a black man to the Oval Office was a big step for them.

(Black children should not be adopted by Whites)

Whites should not adopt black children. Whites are finding it difficult to find white babies to adopt. They are adopting minority children. Is this another experiment we are indulging for their whims? Whites answer this argument by alluding to the large number of black children available for adoption and that they can give them love. They do not know what is best for them, only what they may be able to monetarily provide. The greatest harm that can be done by this alliance is the denial of cultural unity.

They argue that books and being taken to places and events provide children with cultural identity.

Books cannot give a rounded view of oneself. They can inform. Places and events can do the same. Connecting to oneself takes place in an environment that is consistently reinforcing something deep inside that white people cannot understand, nor something they can perceive. They have never had to deal with other Whites on a level that may be closed off from their consciousness. If they cannot understand why Blacks feel alienated, how will they be able to understand black children?

They think that by adopting the child at birth, they can override racism. When a black child comes home having experienced racism, how do they separate their white parents from Whites persecuting them? No matter how much comfort and love they are given, they know their white parents cannot identify with their pain *because* the parents are *not* black. In fact, they may grow to resent the parents they so dearly love for placing them in a situation that makes being *different* more obvious.

They may also feel responsible for white hostility shown the family because of them. Finally, they need their culture and community to shelter, defend, and guide them through what they will inevitably have to deal with on the most profound level of human interaction, racism.

People without cultural identities are lost, and destined to be used as pawns for someone's agenda.

(White children are not adopted by Blacks)

This author has never heard of a case where a black couple has adopted a white child. If there is one, it has been kept quiet. If such a case exists, it is indeed rare. In America, it would be considered *adopting down* for a Black to adopt a white child, no matter what their status.

On the contrary, it would be considered *adopting up* if a black or minority child were adopted by whites. It is perceived by governmental agencies within this society that Whites are more economically stable therefore more capable of providing for the child.

Many black social workers have been diligent in providing foster homes and encouraging Blacks to adopt in order to deter Whites from adopting black children.

As was indicated earlier, feasibility should not be the only criteria in determining what is in the best interest of the child. If this is the main reasoning, why have wealthy Blacks not been allowed this privilege when in competition for adopting white children? (That is assuming they would compete in unusual circumstances such as in the case of a deceased close friend's child/children)

Blacks see the difficulty in interracial couples lives brought on by the complexions of their children. The couples most often live in black and mixed neighborhoods, although it is not unusual to find them in predominately white neighborhoods. The impact this has on many Blacks is not to complicate their lives more and muddy the waters by challenging the system by trying to adopt white children.

The one good thing discovered through the process of people being denied children they wish to adopt across racial lines is their discovery, shared with Blacks observing their plight, that love does cross racial lines and how ridiculous this thing called racism really is.

(Blacks have negative assumptions
about Whites)

Not all Blacks view Whites as being bad people. People in general are decent. Why decent people allow terrible things to happen to others without speaking up is what usually comes into question. Do they step in to put a stop to it, silently disagree out of fear for themselves, or do they just wait to profit by it? This silent majority has stood by for a very long time. It is no wonder the opinion and assumptions made by many Blacks agree with the words in Gulliver's Travels regarding England. *"The history of your country seems to consist of nothing more than a squalid stream of conspiracies, rebellions, revolutions, murders, and massacres. Every judgment seems to be motivated by greed, by malice, hypocrisy, hatred, envy, lust, and madness. You have proved that ignorance, idleness, and vice are the only qualifications for public office, and that your laws are made by those whose only interest is in perverting. I can only conclude that your people are the most pernicious race of odious little vermin that ever nature suffered to crawl upon the face of the earth."*

Does this sound like America? It would definitely size it up. Someone having heard a description about what goes on in this country would come to the same conclusion as did the Queen in a place Gulliver visited unknown to the rest of the world.

On our departure from *true* fiction, it must be said that all Blacks do not have this view of America. Some believe it can become what it says it *is*. Until that time comes, it must be judged for what it has proven itself to be. The people responsible for it are still sitting on the sidelines, as did the Romans while in the arena many a bloodied body lay.

The often retort of "If you don't like the way we do things here, why don't you go somewhere else? There's a big world out there." The answer is clear and simple. "All of you are immigrants. We were brought here against our will. Could it be that we are your conscience? Or, were we sent here by GOD to assure the fruition of the forefather's decree; the Constitution?"

(Whites have negative assumption about Blacks)

Sometimes assumptions are made about people through media depictions, stereotypes, and limited exposure. Erroneous assumptions can be corrected through communication over long periods of time. Believing without first hand knowledge, or proof connotes reaching illogical conclusions.

A negative assumption held by many Whites in regard to Blacks is the categorization of all Blacks as criminals, welfare recipients, *and* ignorant people. All these are lumped together as one because they are most often used interchangeably.

News media relishes showing Blacks in negative lights to assuage white fears. If Whites know Blacks are a minimal part of the population, and they are committing the majority of crimes, they feel better about themselves and their surroundings. That is the intent. As long as Whites think their immediate neighbors are harmless, they feel secure. Blacks live too far away to be a threat to them. The evening news shows them shocked with mouths agape when terrible crimes happen in their neighborhoods by *nice white neighbors*. The truth is, white criminals do commit more crimes in this country than do Blacks, but this does nothing to politically justify false security.

Whites far outnumber Blacks on welfare. This does little to assure Whites of their overall advancement above and beyond other races. The large number of Whites in America makes their numbers staggering in all negative categories. By ratio, Blacks may have an unfortunate segment of their race left wanting due to discrimination, but white unfortunates are there by choice, circumstance, or lack of desire to achieve.

As far as ignorance is concerned; Blacks are becoming sophisticated rather quickly. The length of time they were closed off from information should have left them farther behind than is the case. Unified forces within black communities educate people on a daily basis. Word of mouth is still the quickest way to get the word out in the *hood*.

(Black experiences are diverse)

There are as many, if not more diverse experiences among black people as there are among Whites. There is no one group of people in America with one experience governing them all. Even Native Americans have diverse experiences.

Some Blacks were born in poverty, some into untold wealth. Many were born in middle-class families, while others without knowledge of parentage. Many have been reared by grandparents, aunts, uncles, single parents, and even by strangers. There are also many reared by both parents in all types of class structures in America. We must not forget that many have come from mixed parentage be they of European, Native American, Asian, or Spanish heritage which crosses all class structures as well. There are many that have been reared by Whites in foster homes, and those having been adopted by Whites.

All of the above have had an impact on how people view their environment and themselves in it. When they are faced with racism, it can be a rude awakening for them. For those born and reared in mixed race situations, and within white homes, it is especially traumatic. They must rationalize the behavior of others which does not coincide with their life experiences. This causes cognitive dissonance, which in turn could either cause self-hatred, or reevaluation of loved ones that in most cases have sheltered them from the raw reality of racism and its sting.

No individual Black can speak for all Blacks, or mixed-race people, because of the great diversity within America.

One Black person *can say* that racism is not beneficial to the growth and development of a nation when a large portion of people are not allowed to fully participate in making the society prosper adequately.

One Black *can express* the need for corrective measures to ensure all people within society are given equal access to opportunity, and rewards regardless of race, income, status, class, sex, or parentage. All Blacks want equality in all things American.

(Whites tend to lump all Blacks together)

Many Whites do tend to lump all Blacks together. They show their ignorance by asking questions like, *"What do Blacks want now? Haven't we given them enough already?"*

Since we know Blacks are a large diverse group of people, putting everyone into the same category is ridiculous. When Whites, *and Blacks* do this, they are causing a greater cohesiveness between different thinking Blacks. This has been considered an advantage by many Blacks. Blacks wanting to embrace European types of ideology, find themselves unable to do so because of racist attitudes among Whites.

No matter what a child is mixed with, if black is in the mix, that child is considered black. Black is dominant and white is recessive. Black will always identify itself because of its dominance. Something about the hair will be just a little too curly. The lips just a little more fully developed than usual, or the gluteus just a bit too maximus. The nose will spread wider than is usual in Caucasians, and the movements disturbingly too rhythmic. That is why Blacks know Blacks, and those mixed with it. The *vibe* is strong, and like kind knows like kind.

Many Whites in America do not want to mix with people unlike themselves. Their children have not gotten the message, however, because they are mixing with Blacks at an alarming rate. A great number of Whites having mixed grandchildren are beginning to understand the racial problem. They have accepted these children, some reluctantly, into their lives. They see the stares when they accompany them on outings. They hear the comments, and they experience the loss of friendships because of their child's offspring.

They no longer lump people together because they are now intimately involved in the equation. They have a vested interest in the well being of the child and its future. They now want to see racism end.

(Blacks are conscious of, but ignore white hate groups)

Blacks are aware of white hate groups and many keep track of news about them. It behooves Blacks to pay close attention to these groups because black survival depends on knowing what enemies of black people are doing, how fast the organizations are growing, and what kinds of people are drawn to them. Many Blacks *would* like to ignore these groups, but since they are a fact of life it wouldn't be wise to do so.

Whenever and wherever the KKK march, black people accompanied by fair-minded Whites and other minorities show up to protest. Anonymity of the white-robed hooded racists does more to throw suspicion on Whites Blacks know in towns all across America than it does to scare anyone. The possibility that the local school principal, pharmacist, doctor, policeman, or dentist could be one of the KKK behind one of those hoods, does little to foster good race relations and could very well breed paranoia.

It does not require a great deal of attention on the part of Blacks to investigate what white hate groups are doing. The press does such a good job, all Blacks need do is watch the news daily on television and read newspapers. Word of mouth news within the black community works like the drums of Africa. It doesn't take long to get the word out. It would prove distracting to give too much time to people practicing negative activities. It would also give them too much power over us.

Oddly enough, the hate groups spewing defaming and slanderous messages about Blacks usually are the people most afraid of confrontations on a one-to-one basis with Blacks. Their fear feeds the hate, which becomes a self-feeding cyclical process.

Some Blacks are so sure of their successful reaction to a violent outbreak that they don't think about it. They consider themselves prepared at all times. An example of this outlook can be found among urban black youth. They see themselves as bold, strong, and living on the edge of a system that counts them negligible anyway.

(White hate groups are growing and supported by Whites)

The trend toward high recruitment by white hate groups is no surprise. Whenever there is an economic squeeze in federal, state, and private sector budgets, Whites tend to want to hold the line on hiring minorities, *and* their upward mobility. The fear they exhibit is skillfully disguised as hate. In every area where Blacks have not had opportunities in the past, they are now excelling. These Whites see this, and know they will now have to work harder than in the past. There is no longer a free ride for them. The legacy they hoped would be passed on to their children is ebbing away. It doesn't matter to them what impact NAFTA; jobs ferreted out to foreign countries and downsizing within companies have done to the economy. They must have a scapegoat, and minorities are **the usual suspects.**

Low income and rural Whites begin to feel someone must be blamed when they have not advanced as they feel they should regardless of their lack of higher education and years of tenure in companies. They tend to think the best jobs and opportunities in America are their birthright. What entitles them to it? The color of their skin, of course! When they realize there are many highly qualified Blacks securing jobs because of better qualifications, they either return to their small town havens where they have complete control, or quietly seethe and join hate groups.

Not all Whites support hate groups. In fact, many abhor them and work to eradicate them. Many others simply do not like them, nor see their tactics as the way to support white supremacy.

Then there are Whites who quietly support hate groups. They support them financially and work undercover to further their ends in the workplace, and other areas to hamper black advancement. These are the ones Affirmative Action laws are designed to protect Blacks and other minorities against through the grievance process.

With the possible end of Affirmative Action in the near future, one victory may be in store for the groups disliking it most.

(Blacks can live in neighborhoods with Whites)

Many Blacks moving into, and residing in predominately white neighborhoods tend to get along well with their neighbors if their neighbors are civil and welcoming.

The main reason for Blacks entering upper scale neighborhoods, which are composed of mostly white families, is the desire for nice homes, and better living conditions and schools for their families. These assets just happen to exist in majority neighborhoods.

Most black families moving into white areas do not consciously expect to be confronted with racism. They are not aware of the total composition of the areas they move into. They do expect to see some minority families because that is the composition of America. However naive this assumption, they readily expect to be left alone, and treated with respect. When this does not occur, they find themselves alienated and ostracized.

When children are exposed to negative reactions from their neighbors and classmates; deep psychological scars can develop that cause distrust of Whites and resentment towards parents placing them in this awkward position.

On the other hand, many of the children will adjust by exhibiting pro-racist behavior. They will begin to take on the characteristics of their tormentors in order to coexist comfortably. This denial of self may cause numerous psychological traumas in the future.

Many Blacks sacrifice much of themselves, and their culture when moving to disproportionately populated white areas. Some relish in the experience, and others realize the drawbacks when irreversible harm has been done either to themselves or their children be it physically, emotionally, spiritually, or psychologically.

When there are a few minority families they can relate to present in the area, the culture shock is less traumatic.

(Whites prefer not living near Blacks)

Neighborhoods are all abuzz when new people move in. This is universally normal. Everyone wants to know who they are, how many kids they have, what kind of furniture was delivered, how many pets and what kinds of pets they own, how they look, where they work, and what kind of vehicles they drive.

It doesn't matter what the make up of the neighborhood is, people are curious. The exception arises when the people who move in are a little too different. When Blacks move into white neighborhoods, the added equation is color. Fears begin to develop. Stereotypes are awakened, and distrust takes the place of innocent curiosity. A few neighbors may go as far as to visit the new family to *feel them out*. Others may visit to genuinely welcome them into the neighborhood to assure them that it is safe and all are not racist.

Whites know the views of their neighbors, and they also know which ones are prone to cause problems for black newcomers. When racist signs are painted on homes, sidewalks and vehicles, most white neighbors know, or have a good idea of the identity of the perpetrator or perpetrators. They also know it would not hold them in good stead to reveal their identity to law enforcement agencies. Their sense of what is right is superseded by their continued acceptance by their neighbors no matter how heinous the acts committed *by* them. This is why they seldom come forward.

The difficulty of Whites in accepting minority persons into their surroundings is due to their *tribal* mentality than anything else. They just prefer to be around people like themselves. They have not yet adjusted to the diversity of the land they live in. They are slow to adjust to change that has rapidly been thrust upon them. They cannot remain living in the same time and world as their parents. The lily-white landscape is changing into a rainbow coalition. Some of them feel helpless.

(Black churches are burning)

Over 150 black churches have been set afire, and very few arsonists have been arrested and jailed. Why is this happening? There may be many answers, but the obvious one is racism.

The black church has historically reached out to the community supplying its spiritual and sometimes physical needs. It is the place to go for socializing, fellowship, and a sanctuary that was and is GOD's home. It is still a refuge in a time of hardship, and a spirit-filled place during times of joy. If the cupboard at home is empty, the church provides for those in need.

The black church is the hallowed place where we christen new spirits entering the world, and say goodbye to our deceased loved ones. It is where we find solace when the soul requires it, quiet when the storm of life rages outside, and an ear to listen when confusion clouds the mind.

Someone out there knows how important the black church is to black people. What they have yet to realize is the building is not the essence of it. The church is within each of us, and it is because of this that any building will do. We like glorious, beautiful places to give GOD the glory, but we can do that anywhere. The responsible parties are evidently locked in on causing economic damage.

Destruction of black churches cannot destroy the spirit of those responsible for their existence. It makes Blacks stronger and more attentive to negative forces in the world. Their spirits are strengthened by adversity. Haven't racists learned that by now? It would seem more probable for them to just leave Blacks alone as past racist crimes have proven unfruitful.

How weak the spirit must be within someone filled with so much rage and hate that they would destroy GOD's house. Do they worship in a place of the Lord? How can they justify their actions to the Creator? Maybe they do not believe in GOD. In that case, they are spiritual cripples not having spiritually evolved to understand the laws of nature.

(White churches are burning)

There are many predominately white churches throughout America. Their congregations are mixed with Whites, Blacks, Asians, Hispanics, and biracial and multiracial peoples. They are open to all who may come to worship. Many of these churches have been torched because of their open door policies. In these churches, everyone is treated with respect and welcomed into all church activities.

Some people cannot tolerate seeing this type of change in their hometowns. They would rather burn churches down than see change take place so rapidly. Insecurity begins to set in. They start feeling less valuable because people of color are becoming more valued in a society that once held them at bay. Anything they can do to deter progress, is done. Many of them most probably lack self evaluation skills, so they don't know why they commit such heinous crimes. They concentrate on what is outside of self rather than what motivated them to act.

The sooner these individuals are caught, jailed, and observed from a psychological point of view, the quicker the burnings will cease. We already know what motivates such people to commit these crimes; we just don't know how many of them are out there copying the actions of others.

There is no indication at this writing that white church leaders have allowed the actions of devilish fiends to intimidate them into changing their congregational makeup in any way. The harder the fight, the stronger the power to fight evil becomes. This is not just a struggle for the right to worship. It is a struggle against economic ruin of churches throughout America.

The enemy is attacking from all sides, and America still lies dormant in a drunken stupor. Why are we amazed? This behavior is not new. If the CIA can find spies, infiltrate groups and destabilize governments, why can't it find the people responsible for these church burnings?

(Blacks feel responsible for actions of members of their group)

Whenever terrible crimes take place and are aired on television news; the first thing black people often ask is, *"Were they black?"* It is very important to them. If the perpetrator is white, a sigh of relief can be heard. If they are black, it is taken as a reflection on the whole race. This should not be the case, but it is.

When members of the group commit crimes against society; Blacks know the person alone is not deemed responsible. All Blacks become categorized because of the actions of that one person and will feel the brunt of white stereotyping. This doesn't happen with all groups. Blacks and Hispanics are the unique exceptions to the rule of personal responsibility. These two groups are expected to keep their members in line.

During slavery, this technique worked. All the slaves suffered if anyone ran away, stole from the master, or did something outside the rules on the plantations. This was the *master's* way of maintaining control. Although the plantation has changed to encompass the whole country, Blacks for the most part do not consider themselves beholding to the master in that regard.

Today, Blacks have become so diverse and scattered a group, it is not possible for peer pressure alone to control the actions of others, and neither do they want to.

Do we really want to become the eyes and ears for Big Brother, looking for reasons to turn in brothers and sisters for the sake of pleasing someone else's perception of Blacks? It is commendable to turn over to law enforcement those causing havoc and destruction in black neighborhoods, but that is necessary for the benefit of the community. Blacks realize the less attention drawn to them nationally; the better chance old stereotypes will fade away. That is why they dread hearing about murders, rapes, molestations, child abuse, welfare cheats, and robberies committed by Blacks. The weight is too much to carry. People who commit crimes are alone responsible for them.

(Whites feel responsible for themselves)

All Whites do not take on the burden of criminal activities committed by members of their race. They are more prone to see them as totally separate. They are more interested in the social and economic class of the perpetrator. If the criminal is of the same class, or of one they admire and aspire to become a part of, they follow the case closely. If they can reasonably sympathize with upper class criminals, they will. At no time, do they feel responsible for them because the person is one of them neither are they stereotyped.

Blacks feel responsible for each other due to their extended family structured environments. Class is of no consequence because loss of a few paychecks could mean an instant change in class for a race of people having been allowed to participate in mainstream America for less than a century.

The small number of wealthy Blacks having less financial woes, still suffers stereotypical categorizations, and gives to charities instrumental in pulling people out of desperate situations that are conducive to poverty and possible criminal activity.

Whites are more nuclear family oriented, which limits the number of people they feel, committed to care for. This seems to have also limited their concept of race responsibility. When they see people of their race on the news after having committed crimes, they do not see it as a reflection on them, but on the person. They do not know the individual, and could not care less.

Whites are more concerned with what may have motivated other Whites to commit such crimes as mass murder, baby killings, murder-suicides, and premeditated crimes. A person like Jeffrey Dahmer fascinates whites.

White scientists wanted his brain, and the brain of Bundy for study. The fact that they were white was important in one respect only. They wanted to know how their minds became warped. They had all the opportunities and preferences white society had to offer, and yet, they still chose courses far beyond the realm of normalcy.

(Blacks need white approval)

There was a time when many Blacks felt they needed the approval of Whites to assure they were adequately adjusting to the American way of life. The *American way of life* was considered the way Whites did things, conducted business, and communicated with each other.

Blacks felt they needed a blueprint on what it took to make it in America, and Whites were the obvious example to follow. Today, most Blacks are aware of who they are both culturally, and intellectually.

Culturally they understand that *fitting in* does not mean giving up self, but rather adding who one is to the existing mix in the market place. Added Hispanic, and Asian spices assist in diversifying the all-American stew. One's culture is the true self from the most profound depth of being. Denying its existence is to deny one's own reality.

Education has added another dimension to understanding world theater and how it impacts on Blacks as a group. Intellectual growth has allowed many people of color to share the spotlight on the international scene which changes stereotypes from afar as well as at home in America. It has also provided an afrocentric support mechanism for a people long denied acceptance and approval. This afrocentric outlook is necessary for a people to first approve of themselves without waiting on someone from another culture, no matter how vogue, to justify them or their actions.

Blacks still seeking white approval wish to retain their position in the slave-master relationship. They are afraid to leave the *big house* to venture into the world, and strive for self without depending on the master. They must have the master's approval in order to validate themselves as deserving people. They miss the point altogether. Their birth was validation enough. The world is theirs to conquer and realize dreams held dear. No man can provide self assurance and determination. That must come from within. Self approval needs no man's stamp.

(Whites accept certain types of Blacks)

Blacks wishing acceptance by Whites usually get it because they play the game according to white rules. The key to this game is to smile often (they must always feel comfortable around you), display pro-racist behavior (no matter what they say about other Blacks, agree with them satisfied in the belief that you are not *that kind of Black)*, and be accepting of all Eurocentric type activities.

Admire their art, and literature, and never, ever show sensitivity to racial slurs and jokes, and be sure to frequent their places of entertainment, and worship. One must only date one of them. When all have been mastered, and they know they have you totally brainwashed, an honorary *"White Person"* label is assigned you. This qualifies you to receive invitations to all the affairs as their token *Nigger* in residence. They would never say that to you, but when you aren't around, that is the classic joke.

Whenever they need to secure government contracts and need a resident Black to show their company or club is diverse; they will invite you to the meeting, or party. While *you* think you have *arrived,* you have actually placed yourself into position to be used as the English used little black boys as the Queen's *favorites* throughout the centuries. The system has not changed just the duties and requirements.

Blacks observing other Blacks in this position (such as Supreme Court Judge, Clarence Thomas), often feel pity for them. They have sold their souls for a few crumbs from the table. The black community looks upon them with disdain. Just suppose a race war was to break out in America. If Justice Thomas is relaxing at home in a lily-white neighborhood, does he really think his neighbors would consider him one of them? Hmmm…

Whites need those they refer to as *Judases* to clarify what the other side *thinks*. This is a fiasco. If the *preferred* Blacks are with Whites most of the time, how can they know what other Blacks think?

(Black rage is unjustified)

Rage, according to Webster, is *"Madness—to be mad—violent and uncontrolled anger—a fit of violent wrath—an intense feeling."*

It would not be wrong to assume many Blacks are rather *intense*. In fact, many Whites have been heard to say, *"Why are they so angry all of the time?"* Blacks are not angry *all of the time*, but must be on guard against the hostility that occurs on a daily basis. This wall of protection most often seen in the stern facial expressions of Blacks is necessary. What's really being said is *"I don't have time to deal with your problems* (racial attitudes). *Give me the same respect you would give the next guy* (white), *and I'll be on my way."*

Most often Blacks are not treated the same as other groups. As soon as one enters an establishment, they are either hurried through the process because the person dealing with them wants them out as soon as possible, or the white person is unsure as to how they should deal with the person, or what is appropriate to say. The smart thing would be for them to handle the black person as they would anyone else. This doesn't occur to them because *they* are wrapped up in their own subconscious racist web. The black person is totally aware of this. They may appear calm on the outside, but inside tempestuous blood boils. No matter how many times this experience happens, each time the reaction becomes more intense. Rage festers, and builds to an unbearable level.

White people are highly predictable. A black person can look at one and almost immediately know how the person is going to react to them. They have experienced the above scenario since childhood. When they are treated normally and with respect, it is such a soothing and shocking experience, that they overreact when thanking the person for their assistance.

Some Whites will bend over backwards to treat Blacks better. They are also unsure of what is expected of them. This is also obvious, but pleasantly so.

(White intolerance is unjustified)

The need to be *through* with the black problem is the mood in the air today being emitted by white America. They want closure on the race problem without ironing out the kinks. Thus, they did away with Affirmative Action in California with Proposition 209.

Do Blacks deserve to be treated with disdain? If so, why do they? Have they committed any crimes other groups have not been guilty of? Why does the color of a person's skin cause such enmity in Whites? The answer to the first question is a resounding NO! Blacks have consistently been at the forefront of human rights issues. In fact, if Whites were in their place, would they have been as tolerant and patient in the struggle for basic rights? This author thinks not.

Because Blacks are relentless in pursuit of their rights, and demand respect from white institutions and individuals, many Whites resent them for their efforts. They don't want to feel obligated to treat people they consider inferior as equals. Their programming has inculcated white superiority into them since birth. It is difficult for them to erase mental tapes, or ever modify them to give Blacks the respect they deserve as human beings, and countrymen.

To answer the second question, many groups have committed more heinous crimes in this society than Blacks ever will. The mafia has a track record. Secondly, a historic review of crimes committed by Whites during slavery is abominable. The slaughter of countless numbers of Native Americans, and in some cases whole tribes, can be considered unforgivable atrocities. White-collar crimes are countless in number.

Black Americans have believed in, and fought for this country in spite of its historic record of group abuse. Are they naive to think Whites can change? Both groups, black and white, know a revolution would have been fought long ago if Whites were treated as Blacks have been, and *are* treated today.

(Black heroes are cherished in the black communities of America)

Heroes are those people Blacks look up to. They can be found in black neighborhoods, in the newspaper, on television, and in schools. We see them accomplish great things in spite of obstacles and setbacks. They are the ones convincing Blacks that they can rise above circumstances to achieve dreams.

The heroes Blacks are familiar with are in sports, politics, music, comedy, movies, medicine, and other fields servicing the black community.

Local heroes are the most familiar because they can be seen living normal lives within the confines of the community. Local heroes are held in high esteem because the community feels they're one of them. If someone like them can do well, everyone else has hope that one day they will be able to do likewise.

When people complain that there are no local heroes, they tend to forget the teachers, doctors, bus drivers, subway conductors, mothers, fathers, and extended family members, just to name a few. These people get up every day, perform a service to the community, and most probably encourage young people on a daily basis to finish school to become productive citizens. These are the heroes one can touch, talk to, and receive encouragement from. These are the real heroes in every community. One may never meet national heroes, but in the neighborhood, you know the local doctor lives down the street, gives to charities, gives Christmas presents to the poor, treat poor neighborhood patients free of charge when they can't afford treatment, and has a great relationship with his or her family.

National heroes are cherished because they are *out there*. They are *doin' it to death,* and they *have it goin' on.* They influence those without hope to have hope. They influence by what they say, and by the advice they give. They too are vital for encouragement.

Both types of heroes are important to the black community.

(Whites ignore black heroes, or see them as threatening to their way of life)

Whites often don't relate to black heroes. Their heroes have blue eyes and blond hair. It's a mystery why brunettes do not complain about the lack of heroes looking like them. If Whites do admire black heroes, it's usually sports types, and/or entertainers.

Most black heroes are seen as good performers, but outside of that realm, they are threatening. If met on the street, Whites tend to see them as they see other Blacks. They do not expect their children to place them on pedestals; after all, they *are* black. They just want to see one side of the black performer, the performance.

White children today are bypassing their parent's wishes, and glorifying whom they want. They see *Shaq* (Shaqille O'Neal) in more than his performer role. They see him as a rapper, movie star, and business man when he sponsors products on television. He becomes more real to them as a role model because *He is the man.*

Michael Jordan is another hero white parents can't discourage their kids from idolizing. He has rewritten the laws of physics with his body control and stamina. Mike also lost his father quite dramatically when he was killed many years ago. He became more than a hero when he was seen grieving at his father's funeral. He became a real person for them. He felt pain just like they did. Although for adults this may seem minor, it was quite a dramatic experience for kids.

Shaq and Mike have changed the mystique of the black hero. They have taken him to another level of association. No longer can he be considered outside the human experience. He is knee deep in it.

With this development, we are prone to see black men become less threatening to the new generation of Whites. This means they will have to be acknowledged. No longer will they be ignored. The blue-eyed, blond-haired hero has company. Guess who's coming to dinner?

(Blacks are taught self hate by white media)

Television is the main culprit in the destruction of black pride and self love. It steadily feeds someone's view of life into the masses watching it. Someone's view of who should be glorified, cherished, idolized, and loved. The image is most often white. The other image is the criminal, dark figure on welfare producing crack infested babies. He almost always gets killed, maimed, beaten, or thrown into prison. He is most often black.

In newspapers, black on black and black on white crime is given front-page coverage. Yet, white on white, and white on black crime is pushed onto the second page, or beyond to hide what is not acceptable press. Why isn't it? It isn't acceptable because Whites must not be shown in a bad light unless it can't be ignored. The crime has to be detrimental to the community as a whole, or it is so repulsive that action has to be taken.

Examples can be seen in two cases. The first case is the Menendez brothers. *They admitted killing* their parents in cold blood. Their trial ended in a hung jury. They were tried again, and found culpable. On the other hand, O.J. Simpson was tried for murder, acquitted, and set free. There was no conclusive evidence that he killed two people. The public (white, and some black) outcry was so great because Whites refused to believe this black man did not commit this crime against his white wife and her friend.

Slanted media implied guilt from the beginning, and Whites wanted him to pay for beating his wife many years prior to the murders. They wanted their pound of flesh. O.J. is now in jail, so they got it. The media did not evaluate itself in both cases. It unearthed every possible negative thing it could find to associate O.J. Simpson with the stereotypical image of black men. His membership into whiteness was canceled.

He is now locked in a world that doesn't want, admire, nor praise him. His present conflict may end his liberty in this life. He is Othello without his Ophelia, and Iago has left his sting.

(Whites are taught to be heroes in American society)

"Failure is not an option," is Tom Hank's line in Apollo 13. White males are taught to be the *saviors* in any situation that may confront them. They must always *stand at the fore*, and when they can't, have weapons mighty enough to reach the enemy. They must not fail, because *no one remembers losers* and *winning is not the only thing, it is everything*.

No wonder white males are committing suicide at an alarming rate. They are taught to scale impossible heights thinking and believing they are the only ones who can.

Proof of their invincibility are the numerous heroes who came before. They look at historical figures like Columbus, George Washington, Custer, Grant, Alexander the Great, and others, and see no heroes of color among them. They read about *Eminent Domain* and believe everything belongs to them. They see their great army and its weapons and believe no one can conquer them. They hear of great exploits by people like Napoleon and Patton, and believe no matter what their size or weight, their superiority will win the day. They know no matter the crime, they are allowed advantage because of the exclusive club they belong to. They understand perfectly *who* the *ruling class* is and special liberties afforded them.

With all the above, there are special requirements. First, they receive top priority above all others if they support the status quo. They must cater to their own. Secondly, they must compete against their own, while acknowledging the reward goes to one of their own. Also they are encouraged to work out their aggressions in sports, or upon those unlike themselves.

They are *programmed* to use all methods at their disposal to get the job done with the best tools available, while maintaining control over all the valuables. That's a very big job especially when there are non-Whites who are better competing *against* them. The clincher is that they still think they are the best at whatever they do while requiring minorities to be better in order to compete.

(Blacks supported Tupac Shakur)

This is a very sticky subject to tackle because Tupac had a positive and a negative influence on people.

The positive qualities many blacks appreciated about Tupac were his determination to succeed in spite of environmental factors thwarting progress. He became a formidable rap artist and an actor. The softer side of him was just below the surface looking for an excuse to emerge. Tupac's sensitivity to the plight of poor women on welfare came out in his music also. He rapped about his experiences in the world.

A large segment of black youth admired his bravado when challenging authority figures such as law enforcement officers. His devil-may-care attitude gave them voice against the brutal attacks of police in their neighborhoods. They knew they would never say the things Tupac did, but they could play his music loud enough for white police to get the message when riding through black areas.

Whether Tupac's image was reality, or fiction was of no consequence, he was a role model for many youth. It appeared real enough when he shot two Atlanta police officers he accused of harassing him. The *thug life* Shakur raved about in his videos, bragged about in court, and seemingly lived, turned many black adults and youth off. He wasn't accepted back into the hood by jealous peers, and he wasn't accepted by the upper class because he had too much of the *hood* in him.

He was; in essence, *the man people loved to hate*. His whole life was a cry for help, respect, recognition, value, and position. To judge him would mean judging ourselves for allowing the conditions he grew up in to exist. How many more Tupac Shakurs will die before we get the message in his song? He was warehoused in a place America wants to continue to ignore. Tupac Shakur was just one of many black young martyrs. We cannot glorify him, neither can we vilify him. We must eliminate the circumstances that created such a tortured soul, and we can. And now, Notorious B.I.G. is dead.

(Whites were afraid of what Tupac Shakur stood for)

This cannot be said of white youth. They are forever looking for stimulation. The kind of stimulation doesn't matter. Along with the music came lyrics, which at first they didn't understand. Now they sing along with rap music. They understand what's going on in black areas *because of* rap music.

White youth understood Tupac Shakur. Whether they liked him or not, was questionable because poor and lower middle-class white youth are treated badly by police in their neighborhoods, and many of them can *relate.*

Older Whites are less understanding, and do not *"want that music in the house."* Some of them do not seem to be able to distinguish between positive rap and negative rap. Collectively they think rap is not conducive to white values. They call their own children *"Wiggers"* because they dress rapper style, hang out with black youth, and use rapper slang. White parents fear their children are being influenced by today's music forgetting they did the same thing in the 1960s and 1980s.

Tupac Shakur was definitely considered taboo. The press castigated him with the erroneous *East Coast, West Coast rivalry* (that didn't really exist), the police confrontation, and spending time in prison for conviction on sexual assault charges.

Shakur was the symbol of black manhood Whites fear. They are terrified of the thought of black men *turning* on their first line of defense, the police. They see no fear in the eyes of black youth outwardly challenging the system to *face off.* In fact, the purchase of firearms and firing range enrollments has risen to an all time high in recent years, especially among white women. Whites take the messages in black music literally, and with Tupac in the lead, they saw a change in black youth that sent chills down their spines. Tupac showed them the image of a man not afraid to die for a cause, and money and fame could not repay him for a life of exclusion, or buy him off.

(Blacks who support White's points of view of Blacks)

There are many Blacks ideologically crossing racial lines in order to make it today. Everyone wants to become a part of a winning team, and Whites are indeed in power. The so-called *sell outs* are simply opportunists in a world quickly shrinking economically. They are looking for a leg up as quickly, and painlessly as possible. Their modus operandi is conciliation, enchantment by all things culturally American (white), abhorrence to all things culturally African, association with Whites only and dating Whites only. They may have a picture of the backside of the white person they are presently hoping to impress in their wallet so they can easily have access to it for smooching purposes.

All kidding aside they are most anxious to please those they perceive to have the power to enrich their lives. Devotion to a cause or struggle for a group as a whole is unimportant to them. Self-aggrandizement and upward mobility is the goal. If race can help, it is used; if not, it is ignored.

They will sit among Whites while off-color racial jokes are shared, thus participating in their own debasement. They accept their inferior status while in the presence of Whites in order to glean some iota of reward from them. They must constantly prove Whites right in their evaluation of Blacks.

If they show any signs of disapproval, they fear this would alienate them from white approval. These individuals lose their unity by ignoring who they are, and in time become alienated from *their* group and sense of self. They develop a dislike for Whites beyond that of Blacks with less exposure to them. They abhor Whites for their constant misinterpretations of Blacks (which they feel compelled to discount, and don't), and begin to hate themselves for having made the choice of playing this role. Often they realize this too late in the game. Bridges have been crossed, and burned. Return to that which one was, and still is inside, seems impossible.

Come back home to your people! We love you.

(Whites supporting Blacks who support their points of views)

Everyone likes to feel they know about the world they *live* in, and the people they share it with. Whites are not excluded from this mix. Many of them like to think they are well rounded, decent and unbiased when it comes down to race.

Evidence shows they are indeed biased even though they are at times oblivious to it. When they meet black people who think along the same lines as themselves, they eventually begin to share their thoughts and feelings regarding race. They begin by asking question like, *"Why do black people protest?" "Why are Whites accused of racism where Whites do not perceive it to exist?" "Why can't Blacks pull themselves up like the Asians?"*

The questions keep coming at individual Blacks as if they are King Solomon's' with all of the answers concerning all Blacks. Of course, no single black person can answer for all Blacks, but many whites think they can and should. Some Blacks will attempt to answer the questions in ways they know are acceptable to Whites. They will call other Blacks lazy, shiftless, and support stereotypes that they know Whites depend on to keep their superior status intact.

Blacks placing themselves into positions as explanatory liaisons between black and white cultures to answer for all Blacks are doing more to harm race relations than they can perceive. Whites do not need support of stereotypes; they need correction on the fallacy of them. Blacks supporting black stereotypes for Whites are painting themselves with the same brush. It is odd that they do not comprehend the magnitude of their pro-racism.

Can a man be truly trusted who turns upon his own people? Many Whites think they can, and it is okay as long as it is in *their* best interest. They never want to lose the edge they have over minorities. As soon as they do, they know their reign is over. Like-minded Blacks keep Whites oblivious to what is reality within the black community. In a way, this is a blessing. Information could be the key to control.

(Blacks *sense* natural phenomenon)

Blacks absorb vibrations at a higher degree than do people without tightly based melanin. This natural *sensing* has been the key to black survival.

It may seem difficult to believe at first, but black people have a greater capability of reading feelings emitted from others. Before disbelieving, just think about it for a moment. If sound which are vibrations, can impel one to movement after melanin absorbs and utilizes it, and light can be changed into sound which is done when jazz musicians improvise, then why would thought waves which can travel over great distances be immune to the same process of absorption and utilization? It is not.

The capability to do something means one has the power at one's disposal. The will to exercise that power is something else altogether. Most Blacks perform the feats mentioned without thinking twice about it. In many cases, it is a forgone conclusion that if we admit we are capable of such things, people look at us as though horns have popped out of our heads. It is so normal, and natural for us, that when it happens, we just shrug our shoulders and march on. It never occurs to us that people with lesser amounts of melanin are limited in this regard.

We create toxic melanin by using drugs (prescription and street drugs), drinking milk (clogs Melanin), and eating meats loaded with fats (melanin absorbs and stores fat-- most meats are loaded with them).

When we have toxic melanin, our natural abilities no longer afford us protection by way of being able to focus on input mentally and physically. Great deals of electrical and electronic impulses surrounding us daily are absorbed by the melanin in skin. It is a super conductor. The body uses it in ways scientists have yet to measure. Non-toxic melanin can absorb sound waves, radio waves, and possibly the whole spectrum of waves known to man. It has been proven that Blacks absorb and store radioactivity at greater levels than do Whites. Blacks with cancer should be careful of dosages of radiation given them.

(Whites study phenomenon)

If there is anything in the world that has no viable explanation, white scientists will study it. Everything must be studied in its most minute detail, or it has no validity or use. The inability of people with less melanin to draw information from the universe does not render them incapable of reading signs and evidence of the existence of such phenomenon.

White researchers and scientists have explored black physiology enough to know how powerful and instrumental melanin is. They have found it egoistically difficult to relay this information to the public at large. These same scientists know sunlight is the great enemy of Caucasians due to the absence of large quantities of melanin in their skin.

Depletion of the ozone layer does not bode well for their future. This has sent them to the labs feverishly seeking solutions to the problem. They have begun to break ground in this area by finding what has been termed a miracle solution.

The great MELATONIN is a substitute for what they lack. Blacks drawn to use Melatonin by the ads do not need it. They produce melanin that is the *real deal*. Whites hearing Blacks speak of using melatonin look at them like they are crazy and rightly so. Why use something you don't need?

White scientists are also harboring much information that shows Blacks are biologically harmed by American lifestyles. The most obvious sign of this is the health issue surrounding diet. ***Blacks should not eat fast foods. They are loaded with fats!*** Places like McDonalds, Burger King, Kentucky Fried Chicken, and the rest of them are geared towards white physiology.

Whites do not produce melanin in massive doses, as do Blacks (they do have melanin but in much lower quantities--loosely based--they do not manufacture it in large doses). This being so, they absorb fat, but do not store it for long periods of time as do Blacks.

(Black folks; please stay off television talk shows)

Black folks need to stop going on television talk shows telling all of their business. Everybody wants their fifteen minutes of fame, but like that? All of us know we can do better than that. Most talk shows have become launderers for every conceivable demeaning element within our society. You name it and it's on.

Men bed-hopping from woman to woman without using condoms agree to appearances on shows with two to four women they have impregnated. They can't imagine how awful they seem to viewers. They act like they don't care as long as they are *on television*.

Women having affairs with other women's husbands have the nerve to appear on television shows with the men and their wives. They do not feel shame or guilt. They want to be on the boob tube in spite of the disgrace it brings.

There is a problem with my dear gay brothers. Why are you acting ridiculous and outrageous? Do you think someone is going to spot you on one of the shows, and give you a role in a movie, or something closely related? Where is your dignity and pride? Being gay is fine, but acting ridiculous is something altogether different.

The remarkable thing about all the case scenarios above is the total disregard for what life will be like after the show airs. Everyone and their Mama will know their business. Secondly, some of them will be ostracized because of their lack of moral character. And lastly, whatever reputation they had is sacrificed for a few minutes of notoriety.

Why not go on television for something you can be proud of. Work on something positive and enlightening. Sensationalism is dying a quick death these days. People are getting bored from all the *one-upmanship* airing on TV. *My problems, or sins are worse than yours* stuff has played out. Please brothers and sisters let's have more pride in ourselves.

(White folks please stay off television talks shows)

How many more times do we have to hear how much the KKK hate everybody? What about their family members brought up in the same households, leaving because of the hate and ending up with a black mate? Life is a trip isn't it?

White folk are guilty of some of the same scenarios as Blacks. Character flaws cross race lines and genders. White youth seem to be running rampant. They talk about having large amounts of money to spend on drugs, vacations, friends, apartments, and lovers. When they get into trouble they want the talk show to bail them out of trouble by bringing their parents onto shows.

And white folk please stop having affairs with relatives, and their spouses. If you can't stop, at least keep it to yourself. The world is not at all anxious to share in your improprieties.

White parents, you need to pay more attention to what's happening in your own homes. If your daughter says her father or stepfather is sexually molesting her, most likely he is. Don't throw her away because you *must* have the man. SHE IS YOUR CHILD! Men will come and go, but your child is yours forever. Nothing a man can give you should take priority over *that*. If you didn't listen to your child, we most assuredly saw you on Montel, Jerry Springer or Maury Povich. Your daughters made sure of that.

White and black men, please stop molesting your children and the kids in your neighborhood. Although white men are more often participating in this behavior, there *are* black men out there abusing children.

We are tired of hearing about men who are Boy Scout leaders, teachers, priests, day care workers, coaches, and other child oriented occupations, sexually assaulting children. What is *their* problem? Some of us are beginning to believe pedophiles are not mature enough to have relationships with grown women, so you rape the weakest among us. We are aware of your MO, and will expose you at every turn. Clean up your act and get help!

Conclusion

Politics in America has become a rich man's sport. Congress is mostly comprised of lawyers. Are they all wealthy? Who knows? We do know many of them are not there to transact the people's business. They are more interested in lining their bank accounts. This is why nothing of great significance comes out of *that* body of Representatives.

It is sportingly prestigious for up and coming white males to consider running for office. They can strike rapports with Lobbyists for big businesses, grant favors, and receive compensation upon completion of their terms. After their terms in office, many of them become employed by the same corporations paying big bucks to push bills through Congress.

The public is becoming aware of what is going on. Washington is second only to Wall Street in trading, especially trading futures. The few dedicated individuals hoping to create changes in government for the better, soon become frustrated and leave.

It is no wonder the American public has become angered. They no longer expect anything of value to come out of Washington. Placing a group of capitalists in charge of billions of dollars is like having a fox guard the henhouse.

How did this break down into a black and white issue? It doesn't. We are all caught up in the same web. Taxes are not divided in black and white, neither are services to the populace. As taxpayers, we will all rise or fall with the economy.

Race becomes an issue when one group thinks another has an advantage over the other. In actuality, this distraction has blinded both groups to what is really going on with *all our monies*. Politically, puppeteer experts in psychological divisiveness, chicanery, and persuasion are controlling us.

As long as there are so many diverse things going on in the environment to keep people busy, such as racial tension, electronic toys, and sensationalism, people will continue to ignore truth through escapism.

Chapter Six

Economics

(Black excellence is leading to collective freedom)

Many Blacks have taken the initiative to become educated more than ever before. With this trend came larger groups of educated people vying for jobs within the marketplace. If the jobs were not available at the desirable pay rates, many graduates started their own businesses mostly with the help of family or collaborative efforts with others in the same situation. Bank loans were and are simply nonexistent for black youth.

In the past thirty years, there have been a rise in black-owned businesses by those leaving corporate America. The glass ceiling locked them out of important leadership positions. Realizing this, they have become dynamic entrepreneurs, moving and shaking things up in Atlanta, New York, Los Angeles, and other open markets that appreciate their expertise.

The Internet has provided many of them another realm in which to operate. They have created many jobs in the process of creating their own.

With renewed senses of high self-esteem; these men and women have unknowingly caused a domino effect. Many inner-city youth see them as role models and are beginning to start businesses also. They are vending their creative attire and artwork, opening boutiques featuring African garb and products, and of course displaying their talents on the entertainment scene as well.

Black-owned magazines such as Essence, Ebony, Emerge, Upscale, Black Enterprise, Vibe and many others are instrumental in providing information conducive to black inventiveness, and industrious ventures. This entrepreneurial injection is contagious and much needed to not only push Blacks forward, but also to pull those at the bottom of the ladder up without dependence on people not interested in seeing Blacks advance. Blacks are an inventive and industrious people bent on survival. That has been their legacy in the past, and the beat goes on…

(Whites are no longer in control of black advancement)

"Once upon a time, a large number of people were brought to the New World. These people were made to labor without compensation. They could not go where they wanted to go, or do any of the things normal people do during the course of each day. They were forced to abide by the rules of mean, vicious men holding them captive on places called plantations. They were not allowed to learn how to read or write. Their family members could be sold at any time, and they were tightly controlled so none of them could run away. The mean men controlling them could always tell them apart from anyone else because they had black skin."

Thank GOD, this is not a scenario that is told to little white children today about an existing place called a *plantation*. There are a few people who would say that America has become a huge plantation and all of us are slaves.

The control mentioned above has widened to the degree where control of revenues is more important than control of people individually. **If one's mind is controlled, one's location is irrelevant.** High taxes and various deductions from paychecks is control enough, thank you. The control over black lives has lessened to the degree that they are now in charge of their destiny. The prime reason they may feel they are not in charge is when they allow someone else to take that control away from them.

Conflicts with the law are one example. Another is not standing up for themselves when injustice is prevalent, and not unifying when the situation requires it. The slave mentality accepts things as they have always been. The free mentality never leaves an unjust situation intact. It impacts on it to create change. Whether change occurs immediately or evolves over a period of time, lives are changed for the better.

In America, black people are impacting on systems intolerant to change. Whites do not determine their course. They can only delay them. Blacks are the captains of their ships, and the navigators of their destiny.

(Black's integration into mainstream America cost them dearly)

Integration, in hindsight, has proven to be a double-edged sword. Where Blacks thought it would cut them a larger slice of the mainstream pie, it actually sliced up the whole pie already in black America's grasp. White America wasn't ready to share the bounty it was getting. It allowed slow entrance into businesses, and reluctant admissions to schools. The battle still wages today for inclusion.

Blacks gave up neighborhood businesses to go to work for Whites. The businesses and property were sold that was vital in the cohesiveness of black communities. Where there had been role models for children to see on a daily basis, there was soon flight to better neighborhoods. Where black communities were self-sufficient, there was soon dependency on others. Where there was wealth, there was soon poverty.

Communities fell into disrepair. The least educated became the new heroes and businesses were owned by outsiders draining the communities of their resources, and transporting the money into their own communities. Blacks lost much, but what have Blacks gained?

The few gains realized have come through self-determination and Affirmative Action. That doesn't say much for America. Companies had to be forced through legislation to admit Blacks. Upward mobility was another thing. If one wanted to move up, it had to be under the dictates of those in power. One had to dance to the tune played by the pipers who not only *owned* the band, but *are* the band. Keeping the job soon after integration was more important than moving up the ranks. That was over forty years ago. What is happening today?

Today, there are Blacks in business for themselves. This is the only asset that arose out of integration. Learning business operations so one can do for self is the best of plans. As mentioned in my book, *"Blacks Survival in White America,"* entrepreneurship is the wave of the future. Jobs in America are dwindling. Blacks are applying pre-integration solutions to modern problems.

(Whites gained more financially through integration)

When black businesses sold out, it was usually to Whites or white developers seeking land to build shopping centers and malls. In some cases, whole communities were displaced through the buying of land by developers.

Blacks began to buy almost exclusively from white businesses that meant a better financial dividend for Whites. Black customers often encouraged white owners to hire black clerks. The owners didn't mind if it meant good business in the long run. In the south this was not an option in the early years of integration, but eventually black clerks were put in place.

Black wealth began to spew forth into white coffers over the years since integration. The monies circulating through black communities stopped, and began to flow out almost as soon as it flowed in. In white communities when the money flowed in, it would circulate many times before flowing out again.

Whites gained by hiring Blacks for jobs they did not want, and often paid them cheap wages. Going from $2.00 to $2.25 an hour was seen as a move up for Blacks, that is, until they found out Whites had been paid much more for doing the same jobs. Not much has changed today. Blacks are still paid less than Whites for the same positions, so Whites continue to capitalize off Blacks on a scale too large to measure.

Where pay scales are the same; Whites are elevated quickly through promotions while most low-level positions are held by Blacks. The positions Blacks may aspire to are often given to other minorities (Hispanics, Asians, etc.).

None of the rewards obtained from white businesses are everlasting. Blacks are learning through the process of dealing with Whites that only through black unity can change and upward mobility become a reality.

(Blacks pay more for less in American society)

Blacks will pay more for cars, homes, and items in general if they do not scrutinize prices carefully before they buy, and compare item prices of three or more dealers, stores or vendors. The universal reasoning among devious white businessmen is that Blacks are ignorant to business practices and can easily be taken. This may have been true over forty years ago, but today Black consumers are as conscientious as white consumers are.

In urban areas especially, the average black family is on a fixed income and must spend frugally. They shop mainly in thrift and discount stores for their wares. Show them a price, and they will try to bargain it down to an acceptable rate.

Middle-class Blacks are just as frugal and price conscious as lower income Blacks. Struggling to reach middle-class status has armed them with an astute eye for bargains. They will also bargain for a better deal. If at any time they feel the item is not worth the listed price, they will leave the store without it.

Upper-class Blacks are more prone to pay the marked price simply because they can afford to, or don't have the time to bargain. Sometimes they will bargain the price down to assure themselves that the price they are paying is fair.

Overall, Whites do charge Blacks a *black tax*. This is simply inflated costs for items for which Whites pay less. Whites are offered deals that are not offered Blacks, and in many cases Blacks are charged higher interest rates when buying, or borrowing on credit.

The best way to buy a car is to place two or three dealerships in competition with each other in order to get the best deal possible. Any black entering a car dealership for purposes of buying a car, can be assured if comparison-shopping is not employed they will be had handsomely. Car dealerships as well as Real Estate Brokers are notorious for ripping off Blacks.

(Whites have and own more, but pay less for products and services)

Great deals, major discounts, inside investment information, and first bids on contracts are just a few advantages extended Whites that Blacks are excluded from. Of course, there are always a few token Blacks in the know, but word seldom if ever trickles down to large numbers of Blacks. This is how private industry and government works to insure white males' secure positions. The advantages enable them to pay less for products and services. The information they offer friends and business associates is often exchanged for products and services. Wheeling and dealing is their forte.

The above advantages and techniques have allowed them the wherewithal to acquire more than any ethnic group in this country. They own upwards of 98 per cent of the land, the highest percentage of businesses, CEOs, and control of all media. They refuse to accept less than 50 percent of anything worthwhile and business related. Corporate buyouts and takeovers were specifically designed to make it easy for them to legally acquire promising ventures. They are continuously searching for stimulating acquisitions to further prove their prowess and so-called superior business acuity that was found to be a fallacy in 2008.

The Internet is an extension of their need to extend beyond what is available in the marketplace. It satisfies their insatiable need to be stimulated. Their lack of melanin creates a void that has to be filled. They are unable to draw energy from outside of themselves, so they must be constantly saturated with it through electronic means.

All material and economic gains have not appeased them. No matter what the edge, they still get unnerved when they see Blacks with late model cars, exclusive homes, and high paying jobs. They feel comfortable when minorities are held at bay financially. They see America as their country, and the rest of us spectators of their feats. Their practice of exclusion has made us work harder to excel in this global economy.

(Blacks see Whites profiting off the misery of Blacks)

From politicians to physicians, Blacks are well aware of the many professionals profiting off the misery of the downtrodden.

Some politicians prey on the have-nots to push their own selfish agendas. They use issues surrounding the poor to obtain votes in order to become elected to higher offices where their main objective is to wield power. Self-gratification, influence, and money are of utmost importance to them.

Some white physicians (and some black ones) prey on the poor, sick, and elderly on Medicare and Medicaid. Falsifying documents and fees to drain the coffers of these programs to fill their own is an affront to all taxpayers, and a horrible disservice to those they took an oath to serve.

We must not forget Public Defenders (not all) who do not care about the people they defend. They are loaded down with cases they never get to read, and defendants they don't get around to talking to until a few minutes before entering the courtroom. They allow themselves to be bullied by Prosecutors whose main purpose is to push forward the cattle drive of minorities through the system, and into prison. Guilt, or innocence is immaterial, winning and losing cases *is*.

Public Defenders are usually in the process of learning their jobs, while prosecuting attorneys are already seasoned pros. The money Public Defenders make is minimal. There is little incentive to best defend the people they are sworn to defend. Poor people are dragged into court for minor offenses and fined huge amounts that seemed like monthly car note payments to them. The revenues gleaned are stashed away into municipalities and county's coffers.

People finding themselves in bad situations; end up paying the most, especially poor minorities. Go sit in any courtroom, and watch the circus. People are corralled through, fined, and payment plans are set up with the threat of jail if payments are not made. Statistically, Blacks are fined the maximum, and jailed more often than Whites for the same offenses.

(Whites see themselves as being generous to Blacks)

"What more do Blacks want? Haven't we given them enough?" Giving something to someone piecemeal implies you control what they get, when they get it, and how much they get at any given time. They are controlled by your whims and moments of generosity. They cannot expect to have what they want when they want it, because you make the decisions on whom, when, what, where, why, and how.

Children can't wait to grow up so they can do certain things for themselves. They seek jobs, apartments, and their own money so they won't have to rely on their parents. This works for all people. Blacks do not want Whites to give them anything. They want an even playing field so they can do what James Brown said, *"Just open up the door, and I'll get it myself."* No one *likes* to beg anyone for *anything*.

The generosity of Whites should not even be an issue. Whites' being generous has absolutely nothing to do with the constitutional rights of all people in this country to share in the bounty of what is here. Who are they to stand between Blacks, or any other group's *pursuit of happiness?*

It is totally ridiculous for Whites to declare they are owners of a land that is not theirs. They are the sharers in it's failures as well as its successes, as we all are. Their so-called generosity is a faint attempt to possess what many groups of people have died, toiled, built, gone to war and suffered for.

Neither do Whites have control over the growth and expansion of Blacks, or any other people. They can, at most, try to halt advances, but they cannot stop a revolution of the spirit. For in the revolution of the spirit, the body and mind must grow out of the old and into the new. Just as a child outgrows last years clothes, so must the spirit of man develop into a higher being. So Blacks don't need fish, they need fishing poles. If Whites are not selling them this season, Blacks need to make their own.

(Blacks resent and envy Whites)

It would seem logical that those at the bottom rungs of society would envy those at the top. This may be one of the dynamics impacting on black-white intercultural communication in America, but the historic symbiotic relationship has not been one of mutual respect and sharing.

One group (Blacks) has been sacrificed for the well being of the other (Whites). In such a case, it would seem natural for Blacks to survey the wealth in white America and feel cheated since their free labor was mostly responsible for the creation of that wealth.

Most Blacks do not consciously enjoy what Whites have, although many strive to achieve success with all the trappings. The desire to acquire the best life has to offer is primary in a capitalistic society. Someone once said; *He, who dies with all the toys, wins. "He who dies with all the toys, still dies."* who does not want the capability to buy a Lexus, Mercedes Benz? How many people do we know would turn down a significant lottery win? So yes, the envy is there, but on a subconscious level. Seeing another group possessing the best neighborhoods, luxury cars, elite stores, corporate businesses, and the like has to have an effect of any subordinate group, not just Blacks.

The solution for parity would involve the subordinate group building its own neighborhoods, and starting its own businesses to compete with the majority group, and participate in the world market.

If truth is served here; real confrontation of inner demons must be faced and dealt with in the light of day. Just because one belongs to a subordinate group does not mean one should avoid admitting ones own misgivings, and human weaknesses.

We must stop counting our neighbor's assets, and continue to stockpile our own. We are prospering at an alarming rate without compensation from those responsible for our plight. **We'll make it. We're African-American made!**

(Whites think Blacks envy them)

Many Whites do believe Blacks envy what they have, and will not hesitate to flaunt it in front of them. There are many whites bitten by the braggadocio bug. You know them. At every turn, they will make sure someone knows how and what stocks they have, and how well they are performing. They will not give tips to Blacks as a rule, but will make sure Blacks are within hearing range when inviting white friends into their office, or out to lunch to discuss the latest hot stocks. Of course, this information is available to everyone today. All one need do is research the market and hopefully make wise choices.

The dichotomy of white bragging is the fear they have of having said too much. Since many of them tend to stereotype Blacks, there is a fear of being robbed by the very same Blacks they flaunt their assets in front of. **They want you to know they have obtained the American Dream, but they are afraid you will steal it from them.** Oh, sweet mysteries of life!

There are also the Whites who must show you the ins and outs of the system not because they want to help you, but because they want *you* to know that *they* know. Who cares? Take the advice and run with it! There should be more of this type. Let's hope New York doesn't have a premium on them.

A clear indicator of white perspective on black envy is the way they steer clear of Blacks when encountering them on streets and in close quarters. It is obvious that they become frantically conscious of their possessions be it a watch, ring, necklace, attaché' case, etc.... This is an insult to most Blacks.

The average black person could not care less about belongings worn, or carried by anyone be they black or white. They are concentrating on other things. The last thing on their minds is creating a negative situation for themselves and anyone else. Lord knows they already have enough of that in their lives. White assumptions regarding black envy of them may ring true to some extent, but it is not all inclusive.

(Blacks receive less pay than Whites for the same jobs)

To say there is no disparity in income in America, shows one is highly misinformed. Blacks have a median income of $21, 500 compare to Whites which is much higher (see next page).

When incomes of white males drop, so does the income of Blacks and white women. The pain is felt more by Blacks and white women because they are at the bottom rungs of the income ladder. However, it is more depressing for Blacks when white males and female's incomes are combined (married couples). This places Blacks farther down the scale with dim hopes of ever reaching income parity.

Since Whites and Blacks work and compete together on jobs within the marketplace; they have a tendency to compare notes (in some cases *one-upping* each other). The extent of disparity in salaries can be in the thousands of dollars. For instance, a distinguished law firm hired two new lawyers, one black and one white, just out of law school. They compared notes at lunch the day they were hired. The black lawyer had skillfully negotiated a sweet package, or so he thought. He would receive a generous expense account, a salary of $50,000, one month vacation time, and a large Christmas bonus. He thought he had arrived.

The white lawyer said he would receive $62,000 to start with options after every six months within a two year period, a generous expense account, one month to six weeks vacation, and a large Christmas bonus. Where the black lawyer, although graduating at the top of his class, could not convince the firm's partners to give him a larger package, the white lawyer, although graduating 16th in his class, got exactly what he wanted. His worth was deemed more valuable than the black attorney's. This is not an illusion.

This reality is not only in law firms, but also in every type of business in America. Blacks are being denied full worth of their services. Could this become a reparation issue? Some Blacks think it can with such a wide disparity in incomes.

(Whites feel they deserve more pay than Blacks)

It is not considered enjoyable to be white in America today. It seems as though everyone hates you if you are. If it isn't Blacks, it's the Hispanics, or the Asians, or the Indians, or whomever else there is that isn't white.

At one time, it was a pleasure to be free, white, and 21. Whites had the best jobs (still do), rode in the most expensive cars (still do, almost), and enjoyed the best of everything. Yep, white folks were at the top of the heap. *"It almost doesn't pay to be white anymore." **Yes it does**. The medium income for Whites is over $15,000 more than Blacks for the same jobs, and in some cases higher. White incomes rise faster than do black incomes. This can be attributed to advancements on the job that more often goes to Whites than any other group.

White managers and supervisors tend to advance people they feel comfortable dealing with at higher levels. Whites feel Blacks tend to not fit in with higher echelon staff, especially if they are expected to socialize during nonworking hours. Many Whites do not feel *quite right* socializing with Blacks. They have not yet acquired a *taste* for it. This means Blacks are left at the bottom where rifts often land them in the unemployment line when bumping rights take effect.

Some white employees may be inept at their jobs, but they know they do not have to over exert themselves. They will be taken care of. They know white bosses will not overlook them for promotions for someone black. If they do overlook them, they will be labeled by the white community.

This silent, acceptable fact need not be spoken, but it is being demonstrated somewhere daily in this country. Just look at the rank and file of any organization. Observe the people in the trenches actually doing the work. They are usually minorities. The others don't seem to really get involved until the boss shows up, then they claim to have done everything, but sooner or later old *Peter Principle* will expose them.

(Blacks think most Blacks lead productive lives)

Most Blacks live in communities where almost everyone is either working, or seeking employment.

There are the neighborhood baby sitters. They are needed in the community because, *"Not just anyone can take care of my children."* Day care centers are too formal, cost too much, and everyone knows, *"They just don't have the time to give those kids the attention they deserve."*

Bus drivers are often seen leaving for work real early in the morning to make sure they are on time for the rush hour. Not far behind them are the cab drivers, but of course they are subject to leave at any time with the hours they work.

Post office employees and police officers are moving out at odd times also. Their jobs require shift work along with mandatory overtime. After them, security guards warm their cars up in the early morning chill on the way to banks, stores, and various other businesses.

The black community wakes up to the same kinds of din the rest of the country arises to. Professionals of every kind roll out of bed to alarms, the aroma of coffee, and into cars, onto crowded trains, buses, and trolleys.

The very few *corner hangers* (drunks and druggies), are now falling asleep somewhere, and will sleep all day. After dark they will appear again to hold up lamp posts as they do every night. They are the hopeless who have just plain given up, and wonder why everyone else even bothers to struggle day to day. Their suppliers keep the same hours. They are the few *caught on tape* for the world to see.

The unseen ones, the decent productive folk, are bedding down for the night readying themselves to face another day doing their part to make this well-oiled machine called America run smoothly. If 20/20, 60 Minutes, 48 Hours, and the rest of you guys want to catch *them on tape*, come to our neighborhood. But, you're not interested in *them*, are you?

(Whites see Blacks differently through the media)

Whites have been programmed by the media to view Blacks with a jaundiced eye. Society doesn't help matters when it holds Blacks up for scrutiny in the press, while hiding white frailties. **Case in point:** In Harlem, New York, an enraged man (Roland Smith), waving a gun, torched a clothing store killing seven people, and injuring four. He ended his own life with the gun after forcing the other victims to remain in the inferno. The man had been seen in front of the store protesting with other Harlemites against expansion of the Jewish store which meant relocation of a black record store owner. This was front page news. Since Harlem is a black community, some Blacks were outraged at the prospect of a black business being moved to accommodate someone from outside of the community.

Blacks do not go to Jewish communities to set up businesses. Neither do they feel welcomed in any other ethnic community other than as consumers. Yet, all other ethnics feel comfortable setting up shop in black communities.

The press immediately implied a conspiracy was possible since Rev. Al Sharpton had been to the location to give support to the protesters, and caustic remarks were made on the radio.

In Fort Bragg, North Carolina, on the same day as the above killings, two white soldiers walking down the street, began arguing with a young black couple, pulled out weapons, and shot the couple in their heads killing them instantly. Immediately the press reported that the men did not seem to be part of any extremist group although Nazi literature was found in one of their homes. It was eventually determined they were and the killings were an initiation exercise. This was second page, bottom of the copy news.

These two incidents should have been front-page news, and given equal coverage. When Whites kill Blacks, it is quietly pushed into the background, but when Blacks commit any crime whatsoever, every angle must be explored by those with an agenda.

(Blacks play *the game* for upward mobility)

It's true. Many Blacks do play *the game.* They know how to *act white,* and *talk white.* Now don't get bent out of shape. This is not to say acting white is doing things properly, and talking white is speaking correctly. Acting white means imitating Whites when in their midst. Talking white means talking like Whites to appeal *to* them. As soon as a white person is out of their presence, normal vernacular returns. Most Blacks know exactly what this means. Many of them do it daily. In many cases, if they do not, Whites will not understand what they are saying. Since they are so accustomed to others doing things their way, anything less than that is unacceptable. Franz Fanon illustrated this clearly, in <u>Black Skin</u>, <u>White Masks</u>. Grove Press, 1967.--Translated by Charles Markmann. This approach is neither right, nor wrong. It is simply necessary at times in order to achieve certain goals, or to get one's due.

Sell-outs wear masks well. They do it because they want *more.* We see a few of the black entertainers *kissing up* to be exceptional Negroes. No price is too great. We have seen them offer up their pride, dignity, communities, families, and association with their own people for fleeting approval and temporary glory. They think white, marry white, and become two people. Isn't that called neurosis or something? They know who they are, and so do we. There is no need to name them here.

Children watch as these people maneuver, weave, dodge, and perform quick mask changes. They are amazed at the many roles that are played to survive. Many in their generation resent it, and refuse to follow suit. They have contempt for people *acting out* roles they deem unnecessary. They are more radical than their parents.

They can surely anticipate many of their children forgoing the masks altogether. Is their generation the one that will be accepted as they are, or will they be one not giving a darn about upward mobility? Many Baby Boomers have not tested the waters without their masks, *yet.*

(Whites manipulate minorities on jobs)

This is true in many cases, but not all. Whites who do manipulate minorities are usually insecure, or have no compunction when it comes to playing with the lives of others. Many of them do not care whether their intentions are known. There is a place for everyone, and they think Blacks belong on the bottom. If they don't like it, they can quit.

Some Whites follow the status quo. They silently carry out policies within organizations and businesses, because they benefit from holding minorities at bay from leadership positions. Still others bring in talented Whites from outside to fill positions minorities would normally assume.

All of the games have been played, and all the tricks are known. Proving allegations of discrimination is a horse of a different color. Their historic, flagrant, overt behaviors have evolved into standoffish attitudes, and covert behind-closed-doors maneuvering. Although minorities know what is going on, they have difficulty proving it.

With all the clandestine activities, there is still good news. There are still many good white people around. They are gatekeepers for right. They are in positions to assist capable minorities. They have given them information, tips, and advice regarding ways of circumventing systems, and unofficial policies designed to hamper upward movement within organizations, businesses and governmental structures.

Many Whites fight behind closed doors for minorities when the racism is just too blatant to ignore. They challenge the powers-that-be to reconsider their positions on such matters, and they sometimes offer to resign if discriminatory practices are not corrected. They are the best and only hope minorities have in predominately white organizations where Affirmative Action has been short-circuited.

Manipulation of minorities will eventually play itself out. Sooner or later people have to be given their due.

(Blacks pay taxes too)

Blacks pay enough taxes in America to pay for the total amount given to black people on welfare, *and* many Whites on welfare. The large percentage of Whites draining funds from the system (over 69%) has increased dramatically since downsizing of industrial and manufacturing companies has become the norm in this country.

Whites are now added to the number of people applying for assistance due to exhaustion of unemployment benefits. When the majority of Whites see welfare costs climbing, they readily assume minorities are to blame. The responsibility for the discrepancy is again laid at the doorstep of the media. Their reports are slanted to appease, or rile white readers and viewers to create certain political climates. This has worked well in the past to garner majority votes, but recently the populace has become more aware of how the puppeteers are manipulating them.

As more and more Whites become welfare recipients, they are beginning to see themselves as just that, welfare recipients. Now when they hear the term *welfare recipients* being used, they tune in. They begin to identify with the necessity of the program as a safety net. When they were doing well economically, the term was repugnant, and only meant *those people.*

The political system is unconsciously breaking itself down to its least common denominator without knowledge of the transition. The same people it relied on to further its policies are now awakening to how those same policies are rendering them helpless and hopeless. Some of these people can now relate to why Blacks catch an *attitude* about how the media plays up the race card to the advantage of some, and the detriment of others. We all pay taxes if we work within the system and no one's tax money is any greener than anyone else's is.

With today's economic outlook, surely there will be people of all ethnic groups joining the ranks of the homeless and destitute. Stock and retirement fund losses have humbled many people. Welfare and unemployment doesn't hold the disdain they did formerly. The lines are longer with new faces from high economic backgrounds.

(Whites think they carry the whole tax load on their shoulders)

Many Whites think the burden of expense for social programs is on them alone. They seem to forget that America is a land made up of diverse cultures of people. There are Blacks, Hispanics, Filipinos, Japanese, Chinese, Vietnamese, Caribbean Islanders, and every culture and race one can think of, paying taxes and moving America right along.

The majorities of people in this country do happen to be from European backgrounds, but all of them are not working. Remember the over 69% of welfare recipients? They are a large segment of Whites living more on the system than paying into the system. How about the white criminal element that are also not paying into the system? They are living off it (jail, embezzlement, con games, etc).

What about corporations using tax loopholes and wealthy Whites whom the government said it does not have the funds to look into their affairs so it penalizes the little guy? When do they begin to pay their *fair share?*

White shoulders are not laden with minority needs; all of our shoulders are laden with majority greed and laziness. This is not to say there are no minority people out there swindling the system. There certainly are. But they are minimal compared to majority people impacting on it. Remember, they have been at this game 369 years before black people were allowed to play. All working people should be appalled at the travesty of the tax system, and how it chastises some and rewards others.

It would behoove Whites to thoroughly house clean before coming into black homes commenting on the condition they are in. They may find that their party *at* minorities' expense has caused it to be in such bad shape. Striking out at, and blaming minorities will not make the troubles go away. If all minorities were to leave tomorrow, the same problems would remain to haunt them, and the percentage of taxes paid by minorities would be sorely missed.

(Blacks know what their communities need)

Blacks know what is best for their communities and the people in them. Churches, community groups, block associations, and now black owned movie theaters have been instituted in many of them.

When neighborhood children do not have structured environments in many of their homes; recreational facilities are needed to enable them to expend excess energy and stress. Many black communities have risen to meet those needs through neighborhood churches.

Churches have opened their doors to youth once locked out because of fear. Activities that were offered to members only, are now accessible to all people within the community. Churches are realizing, *"These are **our** people too."* After school programs are growing in church basements with computers, games, and structured homework areas for kids without structured environments. Kids from structured environments enjoy the camaraderie this atmosphere offers. Good deeds by churches *in* a community can draw new members *from* the community.

Self-help has never been lost in black communities. Since white movie theaters closed their doors in black communities, wealthy Blacks are rising to meet this need. Theaters are opening in Atlanta and Los Angeles. Magic Johnson and others have stepped in to fill the need. Many more will be opening around the country.

Because so many people have cared, block associations are legion, and are actively changing the face of many urban and rural areas. Block Associations have renovated playgrounds and vacant lots, and acquired space donated by private citizens. Civilian volunteers, after seeing the need, have come forward to counsel and coach kids after school and during evening hours.

Since people within a community have a close up view of what is lacking, they can best determine what is needed, and they strive to meet those needs sometimes under the worst of circumstances.

(Whites think they know what is best for Blacks)

*"What is needed is more police walking the streets to control **those** people. They need to lock those -------up and throw away the key. That's what they ought to do."* How many times have we heard that said in reference to black communities? Do you think the bill signed by President Clinton years ago putting more policemen on the streets was aimed at white communities? If you do, I have cure-all oil for sale that will cure all that ails you.

Whites have always taken the paternalistic approach when dealing with Blacks. It is a carry over from the master-slave relationship that is still in their blood. The superior-to-inferior mode of communication has become passé for Blacks.

While Blacks may have been centuries behind in being active participants in the marketplace, they have not been totally oblivious to the theater provided by Whites as they wheeled and dealt. In fact, Blacks learned quite a bit and have the inside track on how to deal *with* Whites. You don't live in a man's house longer than anyone else, and not know what, when, where, how, and why things are done, *and* who's doing them.

Today, Blacks are educated about self and know what is best for them. Many Whites do not believe this, and think control of resources gives them the power to dictate progress of Blacks. Uh,uh. The pool of resources available to Blacks will be used for what *they* know is needed not a white City Council man or woman holding the purse strings.

If City governments want to participate in helping black communities, they should ask rather than dictate, assist rather than lead, and show respect for all the people regardless of stature, class, demeanors, and educational backgrounds. Everyone in black communities have a voice. Once these voices are raised in support of positive change, the vernacular used is not important, neither is the clothing worn. The will in the heart and works of the hands build cities, not white status quos.

(Blacks want to meet their own needs)

For many years, the needs of Blacks have not been met by businesses unconcerned with marketing to Black. Now that there is a lucrative black market, they are anxiously trying to fill black needs for African clothing, artifacts, artwork, and designs on many products.

While white businessmen were unaware of the dollars flowing through communities, black businessmen and women were working to fulfill those needs. Since *they* were the first to see the need and fulfill it, Blacks can become successful competitors in the marketplace by buying African goods within the community instead of shopping for them outside of black communities.

Self sufficiency and entrepreneurship are the wave of the future. Blacks do not open stores in Asian, Jewish, Hispanic, and many white communities because they are not wanted there. Yet, all types of people feel free opening businesses in black communities as if Blacks need them to service them. This is an insult.

The time has come for Blacks to service themselves. Money in the neighborhoods should stay in the neighborhoods, or at least circulate many times over before leaving. When outsiders close their shops and retire, widespread buyouts of property by Blacks within black neighborhoods will enable young black entrepreneur's opportunities to build businesses to service their people. The buildup of capital will make them a force to be reckoned with in the future.

America is a diverse place. But, America is also very tribal. Most people live in neighborhoods with like kind. They support themselves without help from outsiders.

Black neighborhoods can become beautiful, self sustaining, protective havens for children and adults. They can become masterpieces. They can become whatever black imaginations dictate. It is up to all of them to take them back and clean them up for themselves.

(Whites want Blacks to depend on their services)

White insurance men, usually accompanied by black ones, can be seen going door to door selling senior citizens and the parents of teenaged youth life insurance policies. They want to dominate the market now while crime is high and people are fearful. They know to strike when the fire if hot. Their black coworkers are their protection against crime they are convinced lurks around every corner. This author has turned them away often. Mailings from all kinds of businesses are flooding black professional's mailboxes in hopes of capturing a market long ignored.

Blacks are becoming extremely selective in investment and business choices. They know their dollars are being competed for by black *and* white businesses. White businessmen also know this, and hope their longevity in the marketplace will win out over black businesses new in the game.

Some black professionals prefer to start small and grow with black investment companies. A split with both entities is not a bad choice for portfolio diversification. This choice aids in the growth of black owned firms, and at the same time allows the investor to realize sizeable dividends.

Whether Blacks buy from the neighborhood vendor, or participate in stocks, mutual funds, and/or bonds; it is all an investment in their futures and that of our children. These funds will allow them capital to loan relatives interested in workable business ventures.

Every time a black bookstore, beauty salon, grocery store, newspaper, restaurant, radio station, internet service, bowling alley, club, or bank opens, Blacks will know it is because they have actively taken part in self supportive activities. They can meet their every need, and must.

White businesses will continue competing with black ones to service black communities. Their incentive is monetary, for Blacks it is growth.

(Blacks want and need their own institutions)

Lack of inclusiveness, which leaves people with no alternative but to provide for themselves, is wasteful in that it cancels out a portion of the population. The possibility that someone within the excluded group could provide answers to dilemmas within a complex society should supersede reasons for this behavior. Since it doesn't, they should be commended rather than negatively criticized for creating institutions to meet their own needs.

Blacks hold such a place in American society. Their history of being locked out of the mainstream is violently long. Everything they come into contact with is owned or made by someone else. The land they stand on, schools they attend, most products they use, homes they purchase, pageants they enter, banks they borrow from, and clothes they wear (except African garb and clothes by black designers) are but a few examples.

This wears thin when their children observe this phenomenon. Children are more prone to speak their minds openly, and in so doing they are quick to point out that Whites own everything. When they attend schools where racism abounds, they have no alternative institutions built and staffed by Blacks. When they graduate college and want to secure loans for cars and homes, they are knowingly overcharged high percentage rates, and redlined into communities selected for them.

Blacks are determined to build, staff, operate and own institutions for self. There is no need to compete with Whites, but to create a legacy for their children. Let it never be said that former slaves did not rise to the occasion when former slave owners were just as determined to subdue and control their minds, bodies, spirits, and destinies.

Let black children's children look back and say, *"They started something that we must maintain and continue to expand."* Black people have always built empires and institutions. In the beginning of time, they did so out of curiosity to see if they could. Now, they do it out of inspiration and necessity.

(Whites do not understand blacks needing institutions)

"What is wrong with what is already here? We have created the best there is in the world. Why can't Blacks continue to use our facilities to fulfill their needs?"

Whites fail to realize the deep scars that have been created by their centuries of denying progress to others unlike themselves. They continue to embrace the notion of superior quality because they are the architects. They fail to admit from where the ideas and blueprints for their institutions derived. Ancient Africans built the original buildings the Greeks copied. Now they claim the Greeks were the original architects.

Whites feel snubbed when Blacks refuse to massage their guilt plagued generosities. They built shacks for Blacks to attend school to keep them out of white schools that had the best of everything. Now they want Blacks to spend big money attending their institutions in order to keep them afloat. Blacks need to attend their own institutions built during a time when Whites made every possible effort to keep them out. When their institutions provide something special to meet black needs, Blacks will attend, but on their own terms.

Should all wounds suddenly recover because Blacks now attend their schools, or should Blacks build their own just in case Whites are infected with another *discriminatory* virus? The overall conclusion is that the breach has occurred and remains too deep. If they do not build their own, they will always be at the mercy of others.

When Blacks decide to create, they are masterful and dynamic due to their inventiveness and melanated imaginations. They absorb energies from outside which *is* letting nature use their minds and bodies to create what it wants to bring into existence. Those unable to understand, cannot fathom how the pyramids were built, and that black people built them. Maybe it is time for a repeat performance. They are capable and ready to commence. They need the brightest and most creative among them for the task.

(Black boycotts are not needed today)

Boycotts are needed now more than ever. In a capitalistic society, the best way to get someone's attention is to cut off the money supply. Ask anyone who has dealt with the criminal justice system, or failed to pay traffic tickets and still want the privilege to drive.

Effective boycotts are unified ones. If a large segment or a significant number of people within this society decide to participate in the boycotting of a company, success is assured. Consumers drive an economy, and the loss of a large percentage of a company's consumer base could mean the difference between solvency and insolvency. Many companies Boards of Directors will give in before allowing their stockholders to risk significant losses.

If Blacks unify to the tune of, let's say, 12 million people to boycott a corporation having a history of discriminating against Blacks it wouldn't take long for that corporation to see the error of its ways. Remember, corporations may own more than one company which means they deal with a numerous amount of products or services. If 12 million people decide not to purchase those goods or services, they have that corporation's attention. Throw in another 10 million sympathizers and the goal of the boycott is assured.

Could this possibly be consumer blackmail? Before answering that question, let's pose another. Is it corporate exclusion when Blacks and other minority American citizens are not allowed equal opportunity which is a dictate of law? If the answer is yes, then no, it is not consumer blackmail. Let's just consider it the utilization of coercive persuasion to uphold the law.

There are an astronomical number of companies, corporations and medium sized businesses that need to be boycotted. Waiting on incidents to happen before we awaken to what we already *know* is going on would be remiss of us. Let's get the ball rolling now for youth needing jobs all across America. Their future is at stake.

(White businesses do not need black dollars)

White businesses do not care about any color except GREEN, and preferably large denominations of it! Anyone with the ability to purchase what is offered is welcome. There are still a few southern, or KKK places where Blacks are not welcomed, but if they could extract your money without you showing up, they would be most happy to do so. They don't want to sit down and break bread with you, but they will not refuse to take the cash.

White businesses need any and everyone's dollars in order to become and remain successful. Businesses thrive because consumers purchase their goods and services.

Integration was advantageous for white businesses. It meant money circulating in the black community was now circulating in the white community. Increases in revenues aided them in upgrading their status both economically and socially, whereas the reverse was true in the black community.

Now, white businesses depend on black revenues coming their way. Comparable black businesses have not escalated at fast enough rates to compete with them. Blacks are now trading more with their own businesses than they have previously. A classic example is the rise of black self-publishing authors emerging because of white publishers' refusal to publish black authors.

White bookstores have been reluctant to carry large diverse quantities and categories of black books. Black bookstores are needed to fill the void. Blacks are patronizing the available ones with a passionate thirst for knowledge of self. Business can be better in the hood!

Continued patronization of black businesses is essential if they are to expand. This is crucial for employment opportunities for youth, and adults. Support of black businesses means support of black communities and recirculation of wealth. Although white businesses need black dollars, it does not mean Blacks should forsake their own to satisfy *them*. After all, Whites do not spend money in black communities.

(Black professionals have abandoned their old neighborhoods)

"Get on the bus," and come back home black professionals. Black communities need your expertise. When people move up and out, they sometimes forget the neighborhoods they originate from because they are absorbed in their own lives. When people move, they do not consciously think about going back to old neighborhoods because they were so glad to leave in the first place. It takes a while for them to adjust to new surroundings, and after adjustment, relax into lifestyles. This is normal behavior.

For Blacks there is nothing normal in America. We are forced to take care of each other *because* we are being attacked both individually, and collectively. When Blacks begin to act as *normal* as average white Americans and meld into society, the group begins to splinter into class segments like white groups.

The splintered groups within the black subgroup begin to react like Whites within their class structures. This means further alienation, divisiveness and in-group fighting. This does little for black advancement and everything for a society most comfortable with Blacks at the bottom of the economic heap. There is no unity, and without unity, no progress.

It behooves black professionals to give of their time, expertise, financial support, and mentoring skills to communities devoid of these since black flight in the early seventies. People left to fend for themselves without proper information and tools will remain in cyclical limbo.

The cycle must be broken, but it cannot happen on its own. It will happen when people care enough to lend a hand up to those unable to rise on their own. Blacks can all do something, no matter how minuscule, to help. What can they do? They can contact churches, community action agencies, youth agencies, mentoring programs, adopt families to guide through the system, write books, lecture, and show we really care.

(White professionals support their old communities)

This is not necessarily so. When Whites move out, they usually upgrade to larger more expensive homes in more exclusive neighborhoods. There is little allegiance to old surroundings other than friendships with individuals. Whites do not seem to be as committed to cultural groups as minorities are. Their main thrust is to jump into the melting pot, not bond outside of it. They express desires to move up in society both economically, and socially.

Italians and Jews, however, are not as easily assimilated. They seem unique in that they move out and move on, but to larger more exclusive Italian and Jewish communities. They also support old communities.

Many Jews also support their oldest community, Israel. Italians and Jews are not readily acceptable to White America. They do not align with Blacks and other minorities. They view themselves as unique, and they are. They are both disliked by Europeans for reasons other than race. They tend to group together like most minorities. There is strength in unity and group cohesiveness.

Strong European cultural groups such as Greeks, Russians, Irish, and recent immigrants from former communist countries all move into white society with ease after one or two generations. Their accents are no longer evident after the generations of children are born in this country. Their children move out, and visit old areas as long as familial ties are there.

Many Whites are ashamed to be seen in the *old neighborhood*. If they are well known, occasional visits are good for the image, if not, it serves little purpose other than to remind them of hard times and struggle. Many of them are also ashamed of their relatives from *the old country*. Their ignorance, uncouth behavior, and rawness make them feel ill at ease. They want to forget their roots, *and* the people responsible for them experiencing the American dream.

(Black professionals have sold out)

Some brothers and sisters can't wait to finish school so they can jump into corporate America, join law firms, medical groups, and the like. They are not anxious because they are inspired or dedicated. They are excited because they can't wait for the day when they can drive away from the car lot in a Mercedes, Lexus, or Porsche. They can already taste the caviar and lobster life, but until then, porgies will have to do.

There is nothing wrong with acquiring the better things in life. There *is* something wrong with becoming a sellout in order to get them. A sellout will do anything necessary to make self look good, and other Blacks look bad. Their goal is to impress Whites. They want Whites to see their star shining the brightest. They undercut others behind closed doors to make themselves look good. The attitude is, *"no matter what it takes, I will get what I want."* When it is at the expense of others, it becomes an unforgivable character flaw.

Blacks placing themselves in the above situation try to stay connected with other Blacks in order to stay abreast of what is being said about management. They need to know what their competition is doing in order to upend them in the end. They also share information with upper management thus appointing themselves *the eyes and ears of higher ups.*

Other Blacks may never know what is being said about them behind closed doors. Realization of what is going on usually does not occur until after the sellout achieves his or her goals. By then, they are untouchable and may have control over the futures of those they have professionally harmed.

Sellouts can be found everywhere. There are black and white sellouts who feign friendship for gain. Black sellouts care only for themselves. They do not assist fellow Blacks to move up. In fact, they will assist Whites at every turn. They are smart cookies. They know the white person they help just might be the one to help them succeed in reaching their desired goal.

(White professionals encourage black professionals to sell out)

There are a great number of Whites encouraging Blacks to relay information to them from a *black perspective*. Whites tend to think one black person can give them insight on all Blacks. This is ridiculous. **Would they ask one white person to explain what all white people think?** This way of thinking is illogical. It is ludicrous and surprising that supposedly intelligent people believe it possible. With all the diversity in the world, it is a miracle for two people to think enough alike to marry and rear children. Placing over forty million people into a microcosm of thought is impossible.

These Blacks are a necessity for white bosses in diverse workplaces. Many bosses do not understand black employees, and do not take time to strike a rapport with them. They depend on black liaisons to feel the pulse of employees, and to guide them in decision making regarding those employees. Liaisons interpret black employee moods for Whites. Being allowed to participate in boardrooms across America rewards them. They can be powerful people. The choices they make can destroy careers.

Black employees kept on lower rungs may never know a black person is responsible for their lack of advancement. Many White professionals encourage up and rising Blacks to break away from their past, hook onto the fast track, and look out for themselves. The cultural values of extended family and friends have to be sacrificed in order for the white person to control his or her life. The tactic most often used is to monopolize as much of the person's free time as possible.

Invitations to parties, sporting events, and the like are treasured and seldom missed by rising black wanna-be corporate execs. They fall into the trap to later find them isolated from their families, friends, and associates. Everything they do is centered on business. Although this may not be the way they want things to be, their insatiable need to belong to the system leads them blindly forward into its trap. They are awash in whiteness.

(Black interests are worldwide)

The United States of America is involved in activities the world over. Wherever there are natural resources that are needed *here,* it knows and will find ways to obtain them. Whenever there is upheaval, it is in the midst of the storm. There is very little of great significance that goes on in the world of which it is unaware. It serves the best interest of the U.S. to keep track of trends, economies, valuable resources, and military actions in order to police the world effectively through the United Nations, and reap benefits of the spoils available to its seemingly invincible forces (except Viet Nam, of course).

Black interests are just as important, but for other reasons. It is of economic value for Blacks to do business with countries of color around the world. It has also proven important to have diplomatic ties to many nations.

The black economy in America lacks white investment monies. Countries outside the U.S. have proven they are interested in investing in black companies overseas in spite of tariffs. To avoid tariffs, black companies have been given opportunities to open businesses in South Africa and other African nations. African-American goods can be manufactured there using native labor thus bettering that nation's economy and expanding black businesses into another arena.

This movement outside white U.S. control of black business growth potential is increasing. The world is now *our* oyster. The effort to change laws now *on* the books to stop black business movement outside the country would mean setting roadblocks in front of white businesses. White businessmen will not tolerate such a move.

"So now we engage on a new frontier." Does that sound familiar? The difference is that blacks are saying it. This is why education was denied Blacks for so long. They knew. They knew Blacks' power of mind and spirit is unsurpassable when *"they get on a roll."* They also know there is no stopping Blacks *when* they are united. ***Goodbye, Willie Lynch!***

(Whites think Blacks are a *local* people)

Most white people do not know what black people are doing, and neither do they care. The information they receive is mostly media controlled. They get sensationalized negative news. Crime, fires, and murders are the appetizers they gulp on a daily basis. Garbage in, garbage out. If that is all they see and hear, that is all they know.

When most Whites think of Blacks, they do not tend to think of them as *international people*. The average picture that comes to mind is urban criminals captioned on the news, people they work with, or the ones they shy away from on the street. They may never get to know someone black outside of casual conversations. Intellectual racial conversations are usually taboo. They don't want to say the wrong thing, or are afraid of controversial topics.

There are Whites engaging in hot issues with Blacks, but they also tend to see blacks as *localized* people, and limit conversations to local and national problems, ideas and philosophies. Any conversation dealing with global theater they are reticent to tackle due to their confidence in the ignorance of Blacks on the subject.

On television, not long ago, three black Professors, and a white researcher were asked to discuss the trend of black authors in dealing with black issues. The white researcher began talking about theories used by black authors. He spoke about a complex theory. He was obviously confident that the Blacks were unaware of what he was talking about. His use of theoretical terminology that would send the average egghead to the dictionary after every other word was not lost on the Blacks present. A black panelist responded with language much more advanced than his, and added, *"My brother"* at the end of his statement. His response was so eloquent, and intentionally sarcastic anyone watching had to be aware of the *verbal fisticuffs* just witnessed. The black panelist won by a knockout. He did not gloat in victory, however. He graciously helped the gentleman retrieve his ego from the floor.

(Blacks relate to minority groups through their pain)

Native Americans have suffered tremendously since Europeans arrived in the Americas. Their stories are well known and need no reiteration here. Today, some of them live on reservations, and others are mainstreaming. From Canada to South America, many tribes still practice indigenous customs. They have mixed their blood with many races, including those of African descent.

Blacks and Native Americans have bonded since slavery. Run away slaves were embraced by their red brothers and sisters, and were permitted to live among them. Both races felt linked because of a common enemy, the Whites. They understood each other's misery, and shared each other's pain. There are few descendants of slaves without Native American blood running through their veins. Many of them are not aware, because they do not know their genealogical bloodlines. A few, who have, have been expelled when the tribe became wealthy.

Hispanic brothers and sisters have suffered tremendously also under the lash of white supremacy. Their mental scars are legion. Blacks and Hispanics have a great deal in common. The bond between many of them is strong and intermingling continues in spite of the divisive methods used by the system. Often Hispanics are given opportunities to excel in place of Blacks. They are considered by some Whites to be more acceptable. This has caused conflict between some Blacks and Hispanics.

Any group of people suffering pain at the hands of white supremacists is welcomed into the circle of pain. People of color from many countries are realizing how categorization works. A gentleman from India was amazed at the difference in the America he found when he migrated here, and the America he saw on television in India. Michael Jordan is his favorite basketball player. When he heard broadcasters talking about his greatness on and off the court, he was impressed by the respect given Blacks. This notion was destroyed when a white coworker in America asked him, *"So, what do you think of our Niggers?"* He was devastated. He learned that Blacks of value to Whites were respected, but the rest of them were not. Did they see him that way also?

(Whites relate to other groups through their gain)

If you want to impress white people, talk about money. If you have an idea with great potential, or a large bank account, they will listen.

Rev. Jesse Jackson has successfully encouraged white businesses to hire Blacks, and create opportunities for minorities. He knows how to make it worth their while. He markets his wares by awakening companies to income potential long ignored. He indicates the huge sums of money spent by Blacks on products and services. When Blacks know companies are sympathetic to their needs, and will hire, elevate and appreciate black expertise with rewards of promotions and the like, they will purchase the company's goods. Money is the key to getting the attention of big business, especially white businesses.

Japanese tourists and businessmen were ignored until they began flashing money and buying everything in sight. White businessmen began flooding Japan to get a piece of the action. They are still there, and will be there until the money well runs dry. They have talked Japanese businesses into opening businesses in this country. So far, this collaboration has worked. The Japanese aren't too enthused about American work habits, but they have managed to remain solvent in *spite* of it. They also like the differences in America. They are fascinated with the Wild West, and anything different from their way of life. American businessmen know this and capitalize on it.

The fact that they are all looking for business is not important because capitalism *is* a free enterprise system. The fact that they are all white is. Where are the Asians, Hispanics and Blacks? Aren't some of them wealthy enough to buy ad space and participate in capturing Japanese market shares? Sure they are, but past customers get priority, and relationships have already been established.

GAIN has a significant role in establishing a relationship with white businessman. **GAIN** is their call to action. **Dividend** is their middle name.

(Black movies with black directors and editors reflect true images)

Finally there are movies reaching the masses reflecting true and sometimes ridiculous images of Blacks. The main objective is being reached, and that is to show images of Blacks besides stereotypical ones like those depicted by white directors in the past.

The new images can be attributed to the rise of black writers, directors, producers, and editors. They have given us images people the world over have not heretofore seen. Dramatic, romantic, and even sexy roles have done much to depict Blacks as real people. Some of the images are still negative, but they also are part and parcel of reality. A balance needs to be established.

As more black writers tell their stories, movies will become more poignant. The black experience in America has yet to be shown in its entirety from a black perspective. In order for this to happen, more funding is needed. Blacks can no longer wait on Whites and Jews to finance their projects. Any black filmmaker interested in getting a story told should feel confident in bringing that project to the public for financial support, and Blacks should be there for them on an investment basis. Wouldn't you like to have stock in a movie?

Wealthy Blacks are hearing the call, and pulling out their checkbooks. Spike Lee's **"Get On the Bus"** is an example of black unity in action. Without *Angels* (term for benefactors) to support his ventures, Spike's script might have remained a dream. Many moneyed individuals are beginning to select projects on their own. They are asking friends to invest in black movies. They are to be commended. We salute you.

The other side of the coin is Hollywood's determination to continue manufacturing images that do nothing for black advancement. Some of them are getting the message and putting out better work. **Independence Day** was pretty good, and Eddie Murphy's **The Nutty Professor** was hilarious. It wasn't a positive image, but we were warmed. It was acceptable humor because Eddie made it so.

(White directors of black movies do not understand the essence of black experiences)

The only director besides black ones able to show true images of Blacks is Steven Spielberg. He has the ability to grasp the deep emotionalism often felt by Blacks in the worst of situations. In **The Color Purple,** he allowed black actors to reopen their deep rooted scars around issues of racism and sexism. He understood the need for them to vent pain not often seen on screen. He could identity with that pain through the eyes of someone personally acquainted with it through the pain of anti-Semitism in his peoples' background.

No other white director comes close to his depth of vision in film. Many white directors cursorily brush over emotions when it comes to blacks in films unless the emotions are fear, panic, joy, rage and excitement. Sexuality is alluded to, but subdued. Real interactions of Blacks in films are next to nonexistent. The blacks are usually interacting with white leading actors only. Although the white actors interact with family and friends, black actors have little to no intimate family interactions, and black friends are nonexistent. They are also losers in most movies. Either they lose, or they die trying to win.

There are no black directors in Hollywood with enough clout, and finances to make the kinds of movies needed to service minorities. They are presently building reputations in hopes of having a voice in the future direction of film. Tyler Perry is a rising genius in cinema.

Meanwhile, white directors are continuing on their course of advancement in the making of adventure and action films featuring white actors. Their reluctance to hire more black actors and actresses in generic roles has caused many a black thespian to supplement lack of income with modeling jobs and clothing lines.

"Waiting to Exhale" and Tyler Perry's plays and movies have proven Whites will go see all-black casts in film. This is an opportunity for Blacks to capitalize making their own. Lastly, the Academy Awards has a long way to go in giving awards for merit. Some people are stilled unset over "**The Color Purple"** not getting its just desserts. Halle Berry, Denzel Washington, and Jamie Fox have won approval through hard work and undeniable talent to obtain Academy Awards.

(Black music speaks to the heart and soul)

Jazz, rhythm and blues, rap, gospel, and the down home Muddy Waters' blues is tonic for what ails you. It is all original music created by black folks in America. It was written out of their joys and pain. It addresses every emotion and situation. Black music tells stories of love's turmoil. It is tranquil, calm, cool jazz when all is well or murky and the blues when things *just ain't goin' right*. Rhythm and blues when you just have to tell the story of devoted love, and rap for youth seeking creative expression. Gospel challenges the soul to take inventory, and reminds us to *do the right thing* because *GOD is watching us*.

Black music draws from the very essence of being. It flows through the soul. Those knowledgeable enough to know how, structure it for the rest of us. They take lyrical poetry and set it to music with syncopated rhythms. They take light and turn it into sound. They take sound waves and improve upon them. They take from the unseen, and transform it into something that is within the souls of us all. When we hear it, we can't help but clap our hands, snap our fingers, pat our feet, move in our seats, and appreciate the beauty of it not because someone like us created it, but because they knew what to create *for* us.

Michael Jackson came along and took soul to another level. Whites call it Pop to erase the African import, but they cannot erase the African beat in his music, nor can they remove Michael's soulful delivery no matter how white he appears to them. We thought they would claim him as their own until his problems with kids developed. Now he has been relegated to minimal star status where before he was the greatest entertainer of the century. They can't take away the fact that his music will forever be a part of the American experience.

Everyone can relate to black music. Without it, America would be a very stiff place. People are able to loosen up, let their hair down, and be real from Moscow to Japan, China to Pakistan, Sweden to Johannesburg, Canada to South America, and the rest of the planet.

(White music speaks to the mind)

White music like rock and heavy metal was created to address ideas and thoughts. White youth's rap put to music so to speak. These are their outlets for expression. Every generation rebels in its own way. They like to explore the deep meanings of life through their music. It is a mental exploration into life's mysterious secrets.

Gospel and country music got their start as offshoots from black gospel and the blues. White attempts to mimic black music turned into black music with a white flavor. Their gospel is more hymnal in flavor than black gospel which is more soulful and free.

Hootenanny, country music, or bluegrass is direct descendants of the blues. All blues is sad, lonely, and deals with matters of the heart, and hard living conditions. White country music is definitely written well and has a twang all its own. Many Blacks enjoy listening to it because it is *real*.

Reba McEntire, The Oak Ridge Boys, Alabama, Charley Pride, and Randy Travis, are a few of their best artists in this area. They sing with a lot of *soul*. Although Whites express their soul differently, in song, it can still be felt and understood. Country music is their most expressive area of music in this writer's opinion.

Back in the day, Pop music was one of the best-laid tracks Whites had introduced. Today it is second to country and western. Balladeers like Perry Como, Andy Williams, Vic Damone, Tony Bennett, and Patti Paige made lovers swoon and romance enticing. They were of another generation, but they are timeless.

Frank Sinatra set many a young white girl's heart aflutter, **but** black women were more interested in listening to the Ink Spots, Clyde McPhatter, Sam Cooke, The Platters, and others. Blacks and Whites have always appreciated each other's music.

Conclusion

It is almost impossible for Blacks to come into parity with Whites. This does not mean Blacks will not prosper through business savvy and self determination. It just means by virtue of the economic gulf between the two groups that Whites are light years ahead.

Ninety- two to ninety-eight percent of the land, high echelon jobs, and wealth in this country are owned, held, and maintained by white males. They are determined to keep it that way. Their fight against Affirmative Action is proof that they have an "*us against them*" mentality.

Laws of the land are the only means by which all minorities can advance economically.

Tight control over national revenues determines distribution of wealth. White males in power decide the percentage of tax on income. Cost analysis according to their collective concerns determines costs, deductions, and in their terminology *whatever the market will bear* in price controls; everyone else must dance to their tune, if they don't, they will take their music elsewhere. In fact, they already have. The flight of businesses to places like Mexico, Taiwan, China, and other so-called Third World countries in search of low-wage workers, has penalized American workers. Downsizing is also used to bring wages down and margins of profit sky high.

Blacks have always been economically challenged in this country. They are resourceful enough to *make do on little of nothin'.* Many Whites cannot survive in this economy. They have never known need. White businesses know the buttons to push to activate both groups into accepting whatever wages they wish to pay. It is an employer's market, and will remain entrenched in this mode as long as white businesses are in control. Entrepreneurship is the death knell for big business.

The core question is how do we eradicate the race question? The answer is simple. If we place GOD in that between place separating Blacks and Whites, we will come together, communicate and rejoice for from that point on we will make this country not only what it can be, but what it was meant to be. ***"One nation under GOD, with liberty and justice for all."***

The Constitution of the United States of America
The Preamble

We the people of the United States, in Order to form a more perfect Union, establish Justice, Insure domestic Tranquility, provide for the common defence, promote the general Welfare, and secure the Blessings of Liberty to ourselves and our Posterity, do ordain and establish this Constitution for the United States of America.

ARTICLE I---THE LEGISLATIVE

Legislative Power

Section 1. All legislative powers herein granted shall be vested in a Congress of the United States, which shall consist of a Senate and House of Representatives.

Section 2. The House of Representatives shall be composed of Members chosen every second Year by the People of the several States, and the Electors in each State shall have the Qualifications requisite for Electors of the most numerous Branch of the State Legislature.

No person shall be a Representative who shall not have attained to the Age of twenty-five Years, and been seven Years a Citizen of the United States, and who shall not, when elected, be an Inhabitant of that State in which he shall be chosen.

[Representatives and direct [Taxes][1] shall be apportioned among the several States which may be included within this Union, according to their respective Numbers, which shall be determined by adding to the whole Number of free Persons, including those bound to Service for a Term of Years, and excluding Indians not taxed, three fifths of all other Persons.]*[2] The actual Enumeration shall be made within three Years after the first Meeting of the Congress of the United States, and within every subsequent Term of ten Years, in such Manner as they shall by Law direct. The number of Representatives shall not exceed one for every thirty Thousand, but each State shall have at Least one Representative; and until such enumeration shall be made, the State of New Hampshire shall be entitled to chuse three, Massachusetts eight, Rhode-Island and Providence Plantations one, Connecticut five, New-York six, New Jersey four, Pennsylvania eight, Delaware one, Maryland six, Virginia ten, North Carolina five, South Carolina five, and Georgia three.

[1] Modified by the 16th Amendment

[2] "Other Persons" refers to black slaves. Revised by Section 2, of the 14th Amendment.

When vacancies happen in the Representation from any State, the Executive Authority thereof shall issue Writs of Election to fill such Vacancies.

The House of Representatives shall chuse their Speaker and other Officers; and shall have the sole Power of Impeachment.

Senate: Composition; Qualifications, Impeachment Trials

Section 3. The Senate of the United States shall be composed of two Senators from each State, [chosen by the Legislature thereof,][3] or six Years; and each Senator shall have one Vote.

Immediately after they shall be assembled in Consequence of the first Election, they shall be divided as equally as may be into three Classes. The seats of the Senators of the first Class shall be vacated at Expiration of the second Year, of the second Class at the Expiration of the fourth Year, so that one third may be chosen every second Year; [and if Vacancies happen by Resignation, or otherwise, during the Recess of the legislature of any State, the Executive thereof may make temporary Appointments until the next Meeting of the Legislature, which shall then fill such Vacancies.][4]

No person shall be a Senator who shall not have attained to the Age of thirty Years, and been nine Years a Citizen of the United States, and who shall not, when elected, be an Inhabitant of that State for which he shall be chosen.

The Vice President of the United States shall be President of the Senate, but shall have no Vote, unless they be equally divided.

The Senate shall chuse their other Officers, and also a President pro tempore, in the Absence of the Vice President, or when he shall exercise the Office of President of the United States.

The Senate shall have the sole Power to try all Impeachments. When sitting for that Purpose, they shall be on Oath or Affirmation. When the President of the United States is tried, the Chief Justice shall preside: And no Person shall be convicted without the Concurrence of two thirds of the Members present.

Judgement in Cases of Impeachment shall not extend further than to removal of Office, and disqualification to hold and enjoy any Office of honor, Trust or Profit under the United States: but the Party convicted shall nevertheless be liable and subject to Indictment, Trial, Judgement and Punishment, according to law

Congressional Elections

Section 4. The Times, Places and Manner of holding Election for Senators and Representatives, shall be prescribed in each State by the Legislature thereof; but the Congress may at any time by Law make or alter such Regulations, except as to the Places of chusing Senators.

The Congress shall assemble at least once in every Year, and such Meeting shall be [on the first Monday in December,][5] unless they shall by Law appoint a different Day.

---

3 Changed by the Seventeenth Amendment

4 Modified by the Seventeenth Amendment

5 Changed by the 20th Amendment

Powers and Duties of the Houses

Section 5. Each House shall be the Judge of the Elections, Returns and Qualifications of its own Mem- bers, and a Majority of each shall constitute a Quorum to do Business; but a smaller Number may adjourn from day to day, and may be authorized to compel the Attendance of absent Members, in such Manner, and under such Penalties as each House may provide.

Each House may determine the Rules of its Proceedings, punish its Members for disorderly Behaviour, and, with the Concurrence of two thirds, expel a Member.

Each House shall keep a journal of its Proceedings, and from time to time publish the same, excepting such Parts as may in their Judgement require Secrecy; and the Yeas and Nays of the Members of either House on any question shall, at the Desire of one fifth of those Present, be entered on the Journal.

Neither House, during the Session of Congress, shall, without the Consent of the other, adjourn for more than three days, nor to any other Place than that in which the two Houses shall be sitting.

Rights of Members

Section 6. The Senators and Representatives shall receive a Compensation for their Services, to be ascertained by Law, and paid out of the Treasury of the United States. They shall in all Cases, except Treason, Felony and Breach of the Peace, be privileged from Arrest during their Attendance at the Session of their respective Houses, and in going to and returning from the same; and for any Speech or Debate in either House, they shall not be questioned in any other Place.

No Senator or Representative shall, during the Time for which he was elected, be appointed to any civil Office under the Authority of the United States, which shall have been created, or the Emoluments whereof shall have been increased during such time; and no Person holding any Office under the United States, shall be a Member of either House during his Continuance in Office.

Legislative Powers

Section 7. All Bills for raising Revenue shall originate in the house of Representatives; but the Senate may propose or concur with Amendments as on other Bills.

Every Bill which shall have passed the House of Representatives and the Senate, shall, before it becomes a Law, be presented to the president of the United States; If he approve he shall sign it, but if not he shall return it, with his Objections to that House in which it shall enter the Objections at large on their Journal, and proceed to reconsider it. If after such Reconsideration two thirds of that House shall agree to pass the Bill, it shall be sent, together with the Objections, to the other House, by which it shall likewise be reconsidered, and if approved by two thirds of that House, it shall become a Law. But in all such Cases the Votes of both Houses shall be determined by yeas and Nays, and the Names of the Persons voting for and against the Bill shall be entered on the Journal of each House respectively. If any Bill shall not be returned by the President within ten Days (Sundays excepted) after it shall have been presented to him, the Same shall be a Law, in like Manner as if he had signed it, unless the Congress by their Adjournment prevent its Return, in which Case it shall not be a Law.

Every Order, Resolution, or Vote to which the Concurrence of the Senate and House of Representatives may be necessary (except on a question of Adjournment) shall be presented to the President of the United States; and before the Same shall take Effect, shall be approved by him, or being disapproved by him, shall be repassed by two thirds of the Senate and House of Representatives, according to the Rules and Limitations prescribed in the Case of a Bill.

The Powers of Congress

Section 8. The Congress shall have Power To lay and collect Taxes, Duties, Imposts and Excises, to pay the Debt and provide for the common Defence and general Welfare of the United States;

To borrow Money on the credit of the United States;

To regulate Commerce with foreign Nations, and among the several States, and with the Indian Tribes;

To establish an uniform Rule of Naturaliz-ation, and uniform Laws on the subject of Bankruptcies throughout the United States;

To coin Money, regulate the Value thereof, and of foreign Coin, and fix the Standard of Weights and Measures;

To provide for the Punishment of counter- feiting the Securities and current Coin of the United States;

To establish Post Offices and post Roads;

To promote the Progress of Science and useful Arts, by securing for limited Times to Authors and Inventors the exclusive Right to their respective Writings and Discoveries;

To constitute Tribunals inferior to the supreme Court;

To define and punish Piracies and Felonies committed on the high Seas, and Offenses against the Law of Nations;

To declare War, grant Letters of Marque and Reprisal, and make Rules concerning Captures on Land and Water;

To raise and support Armies, but no Appropriation of Money to that Use shall be for a longer Term than two Years;

To provide and maintain a Navy;

To make Rules for the Government and Regulation of the land and naval Forces;

To provide for calling forth the Militia to exe-cute the laws of the Union, suppress Insurrections and repel Invasions;

To provide for organizing, arming, and disciplining, the Militia, and for governing such Part of them as may be employed in the Service of the United States, reserving to the States respectively, the Appointment of the Officers, and the Authority of training the Militia according to the discipline prescribed by Congress;

To exercise exclusive Legislation in all Cases whatsoever, over such District (not exceeding ten Miles square) as may, by Cession of particular States, and the Acceptance of Congress, become the Seat of the Government of the United States, and to exercise like Authority over all Places purchased by the Consent of the Legislature of the State in which the Same shall be, for the Erection of Forts, Magazines, Arsenals, dock- Yards and other needful Buildings;—And

To make all Laws which shall be necessary and proper for carrying into Execution the foregoing Powers, and all other Powers vested by this Constitution in the Government of the United States, or in any Department or Officer thereof.

Powers Denied Congress

Section 9. The Migration or Importation of such Persons as any of the States now existing shall think proper to admit, shall not be prohibited by the Congress prior to the Year one thousand eight hundred and eight, but a Tax or duty may be imposed on such Importation, not exceeding ten dollars for each Person.

The Privilege of the Writ of Habeas Corpus shall not be suspended, unless when in Cases of Rebellion or Invasion the public Safety may require it.

No Bill of Attainder or ex post facto Law shall be passed.

No Capitation, or other direct, Tax shall be laid, unless in Proportion to the Census or Enumeration herein before directed to be taken.[6]

No Tax or Duty shall be laid on Articles exported from any State.

No Preference shall be given by any Regulation of Commerce or Revenue to the Ports of one State over those of another: nor shall Vessels bound to, or

from, one State, be obliged to enter, clear, or pay Duties in another.

No Money shall be drawn from the Treasury, but in Consequence of Appropriations made by Law; and a regular Statement and Account of the Receipts and Expenditures of all public Money shall be published from time to time.

No Title of Nobility shall be granted by the United States: And no Person holding any Office of Profit or Trust under them, shall, without the Consent of the Congress, accept of any present, Emolument, Office, or Title, of any kind whatever, from any King, Prince, or foreign State.

Powers Denied States

Section 10. No State hall enter into any Treaty, Alliance, or Confederation; grant letters of Marque and Reprisal; coin Money; emit Bills of Credit; make any Thing but gold and silver Coin a Tender in Payment of Debts; pass any Bill of Attainder, ex post facto Law, or Law impairing the Obligation of Contracts, or grant any Title of Nobility.

No State shall, without the Consent of the Congress, lay any Imposts or Duties on Imports or Exports, except what may be absolutely necessary for executing it's inspection Laws: and the net Produce of all Duties and Imposts, laid by any State on Imports or Exports, shall be for the Use of the Treasury of the United States; and all such Laws shall be subject to the Revision and Controul of the Congress.

No State shall, without the Consent of Congress, lay any Duty of Tonnage, keep Troops, or Ships of War in time of Peace, enter into any Agreement or

---

[6] Modified by the 16th Amendment

Compact with another State, or with a foreign Power, or engage in War, unless actually invaded, or in such imminent Danger as will not admit of delay.

ARTICLE II---THE EXECUTIVE ARTICLE

Section 1. The executive Power shall be vested in a President of the United States of America. He shall hold his Office during the Term of four Years, and, together with the Vice President, chosen for the same Term, be elected, as follows

Each State shall appoint, in such Manner as the Legislature thereof may direct, a Number of Electors, equal to the whole Number of Senators and Representatives to which the State may be entitled in the Congress: but no Senator or Representative, or Person holding an Office of Trust or Profit under the United States, shall be appointed an Elector.

[The Electors shall meet in their respective States, and vote by ballot for two Persons, of whom one at least shall not be an Inhabitant of the same State with themselves. And they shall make a List of all the Persons voted for, and of the Number of Votes for each; which List they shall sign and certify, and transmit sealed to the Seat of the Government of the United States, directed to the President of the Senate. The President of the Senate shall, in the Presence of the Senate and House of Representatives, open all the Certificates, and the Votes shall then be counted. The Person having the greatest Number of Votes shall be the President, if such Number be a Majority of the whole Number of Electors appointed; and if there be more than one who have such Majority, and have an equal Number of Votes, then the House of Representatives shall immediately chuse by Ballot one of them for President; and if no Person have a Majority, then from the five highest on the List the said House shall in like Manner chuse the President. But in chusing the President, the Votes shall be taken by States, the Representation from each State having one Vote; A quorum for this Purpose shall consist of a Member or Members from two thirds of the States, and a Majority of all the States shall be necessary to a Choice. In every Case, after the Choice of the President, the Person having the greatest Number of Votes of the Electors shall be the Vice President. But if there should remain two or more who have equal Votes, the Senate shall chuse from them by Ballot the Vice President.][7]

The Congress may determine the Time of chusing the Electors, and the Day on which they shall give their Votes; which Day shall be the same throughout the United States.

No Person except a natural born Citizen, or a Citizen of the United States, at the time of the Adoption of this Constitution, shall be eligible to the Office of President; neither shall any person be eligible to that Office who shall not have attained to the Age of thirty five Years, and been fourteen Years a Resident within the United States.

[In Case of the Removal of the President from Office, or of his Death, Resignation, or Inability to discharge the Powers and Duties of the said Office, the Same shall devolve on the

---

7 Changed by the 12th & 20th Amendments

Vice President, and the Congress may by Law provide for the Case of Removal, Death, Resignation or Inability, both of the President and Vice President, declaring what Officer shall then act as President, and such Officer shall act accordingly, until the Disability be removed, or a President shall be elected.][8]

The President shall, at stated Times, receive for his Services, a Compensation, which shall neither be increased nor diminished during the Period for which he shall have been elected, and he shall not receive within that Period any other Emolument from the United States, or any of them.

Before he enter on the Execution of his Office, he shall take the following Oath or Affirmation:–"I do solemnly sear (or affirm) that I will faithfully execute the Office of President of the United States, and will to the best of my Ability, preserve, protect and defend the Constitution of the United States."

Powers & Duties of the President

Section 2. The President shall be Commander in Chief of the Army and Navy of the United States, and of the Militia of the several States, when called into the actual Service of the United States, he may require the Opinion, in writing, of the principal Officer in each of the executive Departments, upon any Subject relating to the Duties of their respective Offices, and he shall have Power to grant Reprieves and Pardons for Offenses against the United States, except in Cases of Impeachment.

He shall have Power, by and with the Advice and Consent of the Senate, to make Treaties, provided two thirds of the Senators present concur; and he shall nominate, and by and with the Advice and Consent of the Senate, shall appoint Ambassadors, other public Ministers and Consuls, Judges of the supreme Court, and all other Officers of the United States, whose Appointments are not herein otherwise provided for, and which shall be established by Law: but the Congress may by Law vest the Appointment of such inferior Officers, as they think proper, in the President alone, in the Courts of Law, or in the Heads of Departments.

The President shall have Power to fill up all Vacancies that may happen during the Recess of the Senate, by granting Commissions which shall expire at the End of their next Session.

Section 3. He shall from time to time give to the Congress Information of the State of the Union, and recommend to their Consideration such Measures as he shall judge necessary and expedient; he may, on extraordinary Occasions, convene both Houses, or either of them, and in Case of Disagreement between them, with Respect to the Time of Adjournment, he may adjourn them to such Time as he shall think proper; he shall receive Ambassadors and other public Ministers; he shall take Care that the Laws be faithfully executed, and shall Commission all the Officers of the United States.

Impeachment

Section 4. The President, Vice President and all civil Officers of the United States, shall be removed from Office on Impeachment for, and Conviction of, Treason, Bribery, or other high Crimes and Misdemeanors.

---

[8] Modified by the 25th Amendment

ARTICLE III---THE JUDICIAL

Section 1. The Judicial Power of the United States, shall be vested in one supreme Court, and in such inferior Courts as the Congress may from time to time ordain and establish. The Judges, both of the supreme and inferior Courts, shall hold their Offices during good Behaviour, and shall, at stated Times, receive for their Services, a Compensation, which shall not be diminished during their Continuance in Office.

Jurisdiction

Section 2. The judicial Power shall extend to all Cases, in Law and Equity, arising under this Constitution, the laws of the United States, and Treaties made, or which shall be made, under their Authority;--to all Cases affecting Ambassador, other public Ministers and Consuls;--to all Cases of admiralty and maritime Jurisdiction;--to Controversies to which the United States shall be a Party;--to Controversies between two or more States;--[between a State and Citizens of another State;--][9]between a Citizens of different States,--between Citizens of the same State claiming Lands under Grants of different States, [and between a State, or the Citizens thereof, and foreign States, Citizens or Subjects.][10]

In all Cases affecting Ambassadors, other public Ministers and Consuls, and those in which a State shall be a Party, the supreme Court shall have original Jurisdiction. In all the other Cases before mentioned, the

supreme Court shall have appellate Jurisdiction, both as to Law and Fact, with such Exceptions, and under such Regulations as the Congress shall make.

The Trial of all Crimes, except in Cases of Impeachment; shall be by jury; and such Trial shall be held in the State where the said Crimes shall have been committed; but when not committed within any State, the Trial shall be at such Place or Places as the Congress may by Law have directed.

Treason

Section 3. Treason against the United States, shall consist only in levying War against them, or in adhering to their Enemies, giving them Aid and Comfort. No Person shall be convicted of Treason unless on the Testimony of two Witnesses to the same overt Act, or on Confession in open Court.

The Congress shall have Power to declare the Punishment of Treason, but no Attainder of Treason shall work Corruption of Blood, or Forfeiture except during the Life of the Person attainted.

ARTICLE IV---INTERSTATE RELATIONS

Full Faith & Credit Clause

Section 1. Full Faith and Credit shall be given in each State to the public Acts, Records, and judicial Proceedings of every other State; And the Congress may by general Laws prescribe the Manner in which such Acts, Records

[9] Modified by the 11th Amendment
[10] Modified by the 11th Amendment

and Proceedings shall be proved, and the Effect thereof.

Privileges & Immunities

Section 2. The Citizens of each State shall be entitled to all Privileges and Immunities of Citizens in the several States.

A Person charged in any State with Treason, Felony, or other Crime, who shall flee from Justice, and be found in another State, shall on Demand of the executive Authority of the State from which he fled, be delivered up, to be removed to the State having Jurisdiction of the Crime.

[No Person held to Service or Labour in one State, under the Laws thereof, escaping into another, shall, in Consequence of any Law or Regulation therein, be discharged from such Service or Labour, but shall be delivered up on Claim of the Party to whom such Service or Labour may be due.][11]

States Admission into the Union

Section 3. New States may be admitted by the Congress into this Union; but no new State shall be formed or erected within the Jurisdiction of any other State; nor any State be formed by the Junction of two or more States, or Parts of States, without the Consent of the Legislatures of the States concerned as well as of the Congress.

The Congress shall have Power to dispose of and make all needful Rules and Regulations respecting the Territory or other Property belonging to the United States; and nothing in this Constitution shall be so construed as

---

[11] Repealed by the 13th Amendment

to Prejudice any Claims of the United States, or of any particular State.

The Republic

Section 4. The United States, shall guarantee to every State in this Union a Republican Form of Government, and shall protect each of them against Invasion; and on Application of the Legislature, or of the Executive (when the Legislature cannot be convened) against domestic Violence.

ARTICLE V---Power To Amend

The Congress, whenever two thirds of both Houses shall deem it necessary, shall propose Amendments to this Constitution, or, on the Application of the Legislatures of two thirds of the several States, shall call a Convention for proposing Amendments, which, in either Case, shall be valid to all Intents and Purposes, as Part of this Constitution, when ratified by the Legislatures of three fourths of the several States, or by Conventions in three fourths thereof, as the one or the other Mode of Ratification may be proposed by the Congress; Provided that no Amendment which may be made prior to the Year One thousand eight hundred and eight shall in any Manner affect the first and fourth Clauses in the Ninth Section of the first Article; and that no State, without its Consent, shall be deprived of it's equal Suffrage in the Senate.

ARTICLE VI---Article of Supremacy

All Debts contracted and Engagements entered into, before the Adoption of this Constitution, shall be as valid against the United States under this Constitution, as under the Confederation.

This Constitution, and the Laws of the United States which shall be made in Pursuance thereof; and all Treaties made, or which shall be made, under the Authority of the United States, shall be the supreme Law of the Land; and the Judges in every State shall be bound thereby, any Thing in the Constitution or Laws of any State to the Contrary notwithstanding.

The Senators and Representatives before mentioned, and the Members of the several State legislatures, and all executive and judicial Officers, both of the United States and of the several States, shall be bound by Oath or Affirmation, to support this Constitution; but no religious Test shall ever be required as a Qualification to any Office or public Trust under the United States.

ARTICLE VII---Ratification

The Ratification of the Conventions of nine States, shall be sufficient for the Establishment of this Constitution between the States so ratifying the Same.

Done in Convention by the Unanimous Consent of the States present the Seventeenth Day of September in the Year of our Lord one thousand seven hundred and Eighty seven and of the Independence of the United States of America the Twelfth In Witness whereof We have hereunto subscribed our Names,

G_. Washington---Presidt. And deputy from Virginia

New Hampshire	John Langdon, Nicholas Gilman
Massachusetts	Nathaniel Gorham, Rufus King
Connecticut	Wm. Saml. Johnson, Roger Sherman
New York	Alexander Hamilton
New Jersey	Wil: Livingston, David Brearley, Wm. Paterson, Jona: Dayton
Pennsylvania	B Franklin, Thomas Mifflin, Robt Morris, Geo. Clymer, Thos. FitzSimons, Jared Ingersoll, James Wilson, Gouv Morris
Delaware	Geo: Read, Gunning Bedford jun, John Dickinson, Richard Bassett, Jaco: Broom
Maryland	James McHenry, Dan of St Thos. Jenifer, Danl Carroll
Virginia	John Blair---, James Madison Jr.

Richd. Dobbs
Spaight
Hu Williamson

North Carolina   Wm. Blount

South Carolina   J. Rutledge
Charles
Cotesworth
Pinckney
Charles
Pinckney
Pierce Butler

Georgia William Few
Abr Baldwin

Attest William Jackson Secretary

In Convention Monday September 17th 1787. Present The States of

New Hampshire, Massachusetts, Connecticut, Mr. Hamilton from New York, New Jersey, Pennsylvania, Delaware, Maryland, Virginia, North Carolina, South Carolina and Georgia.

Resolved,

That the preceeding Constitution be laid before the United States in Congress assembled, and that it is the Opinion of this Convention, that it should afterwards be submitted to a Convention of Delegates, chosen in each State by the People thereof, under the Recommendation of its Legislature, for their Assent and Ratification; and

that each Convention assenting to and ratifying the Same, should give Notice thereof to the United States in Congress assembled. Resolved, That it is the Opinion of the Convention, that as soon as the Conventions of nine States shall have ratified this Constitution, the United States in Congress assembled should fix a Day on which Electors should be appointed by the States which shall have ratified the same, and a Day on which the Electors should assemble to vote for the President, and the Time and Place for commencing proceedings under this Constitution.

That after such Publication the Electors should be appointed, and the Senators and Representatives elected: That the Electors should meet on the Day fixed for the Election of the President, and should transmit their Votes certified, signed sealed and directed, as the Constitution requires, to the Secretary of the United States in Congress assembled, that the Senators and Representatives should convene at the Time and Place assigned; that the Senators should appoint a President of the Senate, for the sole Purpose of receiving, opening and counting the Votes for President; and, that after he shall be chosen, the Congress, together with the President, should, without Delay, proceed to execute this Constitution.

By the unanimous Order of the Convention

G_. Washington---Presidt.

W. JACKSON Secretary

*Congress of The United States

begun and held at the City of New York,
on Wednesday the fourth of March,
one thousand seven hundred and
eighty nine

The Conventions of a number of the States, having at the time of their adopting the Constitution, expressed a desire, in order to prevent misconstruction or abuse of its powers, that further declaratory and restrictive clauses should be added: And as extending the ground of public confidence in the Government, will best ensure the beneficent ends of its institution:

RESOLVED by the Senate and House of Representatives of the United States of America, in Congress assembled, two thirds of both Houses concurring, that the following Articles be proposed to the Legislatures of the several States, as Amendments to the Constitution of the United States, all or any of which Articles, when ratified by three fourths of the said Legislatures, to be valid to all intents and purposes, as part of the said Constitution; viz.t.

ARTICLES in addition to, and Amendment of the Constitution of the United States of America, proposed by Congress, and ratified by the Legislatures of the several States pursuant to the fifth Article of the original Constitution....

Frederick Augustus Muhlenberg
Speaker of the House of Representatives.

John Adams, Vice-President of the United States, and President of the Senate.

ATTEST,
JOHN BECKLEY, Clerk of the House of Representatives.
SAM A. OTIS Secretary of the Senate.

* On September 25, 1789, Congress transmitted to the state legislatures twelve proposed amendments, two of which, having to do with Congressional representation and Congressional pay, were not adopted. The remaining ten amendments became the Bill of Rights.

AMENDMENTS
TO THE CONSTITUTION
OF THE
UNITED STATES OF AMERICA

(FIRST 10 Amendments = BILL OF RIGHTS)

Amendment 1--Religion, Speech, Assembly, Politics

Congress shall make no law respecting an establish-ment of religion, or prohibiting the free exercise thereof; or abridging the freedom of speech, or of the press, or the right of the people peaceably to assemble, and to petition the Government for a redress of grievances.

Amendment 2--Militia & Right to Bear Arms

A well regulated Militia, being necessary to the security of a free State, the right of the people to keep and bear Arms, shall not be infringed.

Amendment 3--Soldiers/Quartering

No Soldier shall, in time of peace be quartered in any house, without the consent of the Owner, nor in time of war, but in a manner to be prescribed by law.

Amendment 4--Searches & Seizures

The right of the people to be secure in their persons, houses, papers, and effects, against unreason-
able searches and seizures, shall not be violated, and no Warrants shall issue, but upon probable cause, supported by Oath or affirmation, and particularly describing the place to be searched, and the persons or things to be seized.

Amendment 5--Grand Juries, Double Jeopardy, Due Process, Self-Incrimination & Eminent Domain

No person shall be held to answer for a capital, or otherwise infamous crime, unless on a presentment or indictment of a Grand Jury, except in cases arising in the land or naval forces, or in the Militia, when in actual service in time of War or public danger; nor shall any person be subject for the same offence to be twice put in jeopardy of life or limb, nor shall be compelled in any criminal case to be a witness against himself, nor be deprived of life, liberty, or property, without due process of law; nor shall private property be taken for public use without just compensation.

Amendment 6--Criminal Courts

In all criminal prosecutions, the accused shall enjoy the right to a speedy and public trial, by an impartial jury of the State and district wherein the crime shall have been committed; which district shall have been previously ascertained by law, and to be informed of the nature and cause of the accusation; to be confronted with the witnesses against him; to have compulsory process for obtaining witnesses in his favor, and to have the assistance of counsel for his defence.

Amendment 7--Trial by Jury/ Common Law

In Suits at common law, where the value in controversy shall exceed twenty dollars, the right of trial by jury shall be preserved, and no fact tried by a jury, shall be otherwise reexamined in any Court of the United States, than according to the rules of the common law.

Amendment 8--Bail, Cruel, and Unusual Punishment

Excessive bail shall not be required, nor excessive fines imposed, nor cruel and unusual punishments inflicted.

Amendment 9--Rights Retained/ People

The enumeration in the Constitution of certain rights shall not be construed to deny or disparage others retained by the people.

Amendment 10--Reserved Powers of the State

The powers not delegated to the United States by the Constitution, nor prohibited by it to the States, are reserved to the States respectively, or to the people.

(END OF THE BILL OF RIGHTS)

Amendment 11--Suits Against The States

(Ratified February 7, 1795)

The Judicial power of the United States shall not be construed to extend to any suit in law or equity, commenced or prosecuted against one of the United States by Citizens of another State, or by Citizens or Subjects of any Foreign State.

Amendment 12--Election of the President

(Ratified June 15, 1804)

The Electors shall meet in their respective states, and vote by ballot for President and Vice President, one of whom, at least, shall not be an inhabitant of the same state with themselves; they shall name in their ballots the person voted for as President, and in distinct ballots the person voted for as Vice-President, and they shall make distinct lists of all persons voted for as President, and of all persons voted for as Vice-President, and of the number of votes for each, which lists they shall sign and certify, and transmit sealed to the seat of the government of the United States, directed to the President of the Senate;--The President of the Senate shall, in the presence of the Senate and House of Representatives, open all the certificates and the votes shall then be counted; The person having the greatest number of votes for President, shall be the President, if such number be a majority of the whole number of Electors appointed; and if no person have such majority, then from the persons having the highest numbers not exceeding three on the list of those voted for as President, the House of Representatives shall choose immediately, by ballot, the President. But in choosing the President, the votes shall be taken by states, the representation from each state having one vote; a quorum for this purpose shall consist of a member or members from two-thirds of the states, and a majority of all the states shall be necessary to a choice. [And if the House of Representatives shall not choose a President whenever the right of choice shall devolve upon them, before the fourth day of March next following, then the Vice-President shall act as President, as in the case of the death or other constitutional disability of the President---][12] The person having the greatest number of votes as Vice-President, shall be the the Vice-President, if such number be a majority of the whole number of Electors appointed, and if no person have a majority, then from the two highest numbers on the list, the Senate shall choose the Vice-President; a quorum for the purpose shall consist of two-thirds of the whole number of Senators, and a majority of the

---

[12] Changed by the 20th Amendment

whole number shall be necessary to a choice. But no person constitutionally ineligible to the office of President shall be eligible to that of Vice-President of the United States.

Amendment 13--Prohibition of Slavery

(Ratified December 6, 1865)

Section 1. Neither slavery nor involuntary servitude, except as a punishment for crime whereof the party shall have been duly convicted, shall exist within the United States, or any place subject to their jurisdiction.

Section 2. Congress shall have power to enforce this article by appropriate legislation.

Amendment 14--Citizenship, Due Process, & Equal Protection of the Laws

(Ratified July 9, 1868)

Section 1. All persons born or naturalized in the United States and subject to the jurisdiction thereof, are citizens of the United States and of the State wherein they reside. No State shall make or enforce any law which shall abridge the privileges or immunities of citizens of the United States; nor shall any State deprive any person of life, liberty, or property, without due process of law; nor deny to any person within its jurisdiction the equal protection of the laws.

Section 2. Representatives shall be apportioned among the several States according to their respective numbers, counting the whole number of persons in each State, excluding Indians not taxed. But when the right to vote at any election for the choice of electors for President and Vice President of the United States, Representatives in Congress, the Executive and Judicial officers of a State, or the members of the Legislature thereof, is denied to any of the male inhabitants of such State, being [twenty-one][13] years of age, and citizens of the United States, or in any way abridged, except for participation in rebellion, or other crime, the basis of representation therein shall be reduced in the proportion which the number of such male citizens shall bear to the whole number of male citizens twenty-one years of age in such State.

Section 3. No person shall be a Senator or Representative in Congress, or elector of President and Vice President, or hold any office, civil or military, under the United States, or under any State, who, having previously taken an oath, as a member of Congress, or as an officer of the United States, or as a member of any State Legislature, or as an executive or judicial officer of any State, to support the Constitution of the United States, shall have engaged in insurrection or rebellion against the same, or given aid or comfort to the enemies thereof. But Congress may by a vote of two-thirds of each House, remove such disability.

Section 4. The validity of the public debt of the United States, authorized by law, including debts incurred for payment of pensions and bounties for services in suppressing insurrection or rebellion, shall not be questioned. But neither the United States nor any State shall assume or pay any debt or obligation incurred in aid of

---

[13] Changed by the 26th Amendment

insurrection or rebellion against the United States, or any claim for the loss or emancipation of any slave; but all such debts, obligations and claims shall be held illegal and void.

Section 5. The Congress shall have power to enforce, by appropriate legislation, the provisions of this article.

Amendment 15--Right To Vote

(Ratified February 3, 1870)

Section 1. The right of citizens of the United States to vote shall not be denied or abridged by the United States or by any State on account of race, color, or previous condition of servitude.

Section 2. The Congress shall have power to enforce this article by appropriate legislation.

Amendment 16--Income Taxes

(Ratified February 3, 1913)

The Congress shall have power to lay and collect taxes on incomes, from whatever source derived, without apportionment among the several States, and without regard to any census or enumeration.

Amendment 17--Election of Senators

(Ratified April 8, 1913)

The Senate of the United States shall be composed of two Senators from each State, elected by the people thereof, for six years; and each Senator shall have one vote. The elector in each State shall have the qualifications requisite for electors of the most numerous branch of the State legislatures.

When vacancies happen in the representation of any State in the Senate, the executive authority of such State shall issue writs of election to fill such vacancies: *Provided*, That the legislature of any State may empower the executive thereof to make temporary appointments until the people fill the vacancies by election as the legislature may direct.

This amendment shall not be so construed as to affect the election or term of any Senator chosen before it becomes valid as part of the Constitution.

Amendment 18--Prohibition

(Ratified January 16, 1919)

[*Section 1.* After one year from the ratification of this article the manufacture, sale, or transportation of intoxicating liquors within, the importation thereof into, or the exportation thereof from the United States and all territory subject to the jurisdiction thereof for beverage purposes is hereby prohibited.

Section 2. The Congress and the several States shall have concurrent power to enforce this article by appropriate legislation.

Section 3. This article shall be inoperative unless it shall have been ratified as an amendment to the Constitution by the legislatures of the several States, as provided in the Constitution, within seven years from the date of the submission hereof to the States by the Congress.][14]

Amendment 19--Woman's Suffrage

(Ratified August 18, 1920)

The right of citizens of the United States to vote shall not be denied or abridged by the United States or by any State on account of sex.

Congress shall have power to enforce this article by appropriate legislation.

Amendment 20--Lame Duck Amendment

(Ratified January 23, 1933)

Section 1. The term of the President and Vice President shall end at noon on the 20th day of January, and the terms of Senators and Representatives at noon on the 3rd day of January, of the years in which such terms would have ended if this article had not been ratified; and the terms of their successor shall then begin.

Section 2. The Congress shall assemble at least once in every year, and such meeting shall begin at noon on the 3rd day of January, unless they shall by law appoint a different day.

Section 3. If, at the time fixed for the beginning of the term of the President, the President elect shall have died, the Vice President elect shall become President. If a President shall not have been chosen before the time fixed for the beginning of his term, or if the President elect shall have failed

---

to qualify, then the Vice President elect shall act as President until a President shall have qualified; and the Congress may by law provide for the case wherein neither a President elect nor a Vice President elect shall have qualified, declaring who shall then act as President, or the manner in which one who is to act shall be selected, and such person shall act accordingly until a President or Vice President shall have qualified.

Section 4. The Congress may by law provide for the case of the death of any of the persons from whom the House of Representatives may choose a President whenever the right of choice shall have devolved upon them, and for the case of the death of any of the persons from whom the Senate may choose a Vice President whenever the right of choice shall have devolved upon them.

Section 5. Sections 1 and 2 shall take effect on the 15th day of October following the ratification of this article.

Section 6. This article shall be inoperative unless it shall have been ratified as an amendment to the Constitution by the legislatures of three-fourths of the several States within seven years from the date of its submission.

Amendment 21--Repeal of Prohibition

(Ratified December 5, 1933)

Section 1. The eighteenth article of amendment to the Constitution of the United States is hereby repealed.

Section 2. The transportation or importation into any State, Territory,

---

[14] The 18th Amendment was repealed by the 21st Amendment, December 5, 1933.

or possession of the United States for delivery or use therein of intoxicating liquors, in violation of the laws thereof, is hereby prohibited.

Section 3. This article shall be inoperative unless it shall have been ratified as an amendment to the Constitution by conventions in the several States, as provided in the Constitution, within seven years from the date of the submission hereof to the States by the Congress.

Amendment 22--Presidential Terms

(Ratified February 27, 1951)

Section 1. No person shall be elected to the office of the President more than twice, and no person who has held the office of President, or acted as President, for more than two years of a term to which some other person was elected President shall be elected to the office of the President more than once. But this Article shall not apply to any person holding the office of President when this Article was proposed by the Congress, and shall not prevent any person who may be holding the office of President, or acting as President, during the term within which this Article becomes operative from holding the office of President or acting as President during the remainder of such term.

Section 2. This article shall be inoperative unless it shall have been ratified as an amendment to the Constitution by the legislatures of three-fourths of the several States within seven years from the date of its submission to the States by the Congress.

Amendment 23--District of Columbia/ Presidential Electors

(Ratified March 29, 1961)

Section 1. The District constituting the seat of Government of the United States shall appoint in such manner as the Congress may direct:

A number of electors of President and Vice President equal to the whole number of Senators and Representatives in Congress to which the District would be entitled if it were a State, but in no event more than the least populous State; they shall be in addition to those appointed by the States, but they shall be considered, for the purposes of the election of President and Vice President, to be electors appointed by a State; and they shall meet in the District and perform such duties as provided by the twelfth article of amendment.

Section 2. The Congress shall have power to enforce this article by appropriate legislation.

Amendment 24--Anti-Poll Tax

(Ratified January 23, 1964)

Section 1. The right of citizens of the United States to vote in any primary or other election for President or Vice President, for electors for President or Vice President, or for Senator or Representative in Congress, shall not be denied or abridged by the United States or any State by reason of failure to pay any poll tax or other tax.

Section 2. The Congress shall have power to enforce this article by appropriate legislation.

Amendment 25--Presidential Disability/Vice Presidential Vacancies

(Ratified February 10, 1967)

Section 1. In case of the removal of the President from office or of his death or resignation, the Vice President shall become President.

Section 2. Whenever there is a vacancy in the office of the Vice President, the President shall nominate a Vice President, who shall take office upon confirmation by a majority vote of both Houses of Congress.

Section 3. Whenever the President transmits to the President pro tempore of the Senate and the Speaker of the House of Representatives his written declaration that he is unable to discharge the powers and duties of his office, and until he transmits to them a written declaration to the contrary, such powers and duties shall be discharged by the Vice President as Acting President.

Section 4. Whenever the Vice President and a majority of either the principal officers of the executive departments or of such other body as Congress may by law provide, transmit to the President pro tempore of the Senate and the Speaker of the House of Representatives their written declaration that the President is unable to discharge the powers and duties of his office, the Vice President shall immediately assume the powers and duties of the office as Acting President.

Thereafter, when the President transmits to the President pro tempore of the Senate and the Speaker of the House of Representatives his written declaration that no inability exists, he shall resume the powers and duties of his office unless the Vice President and a majority of either the principal officers of the executive department or of such other body as Congress may by law provide, transmit within four days to the President pro tempore of the Senate and the Speaker of the House of Representatives their written declaration that the President is unable to discharge the powers and duties of his office. Thereupon Congress shall decide the issue, assembling within forty-eight hours for that purpose if not in session,. If the Congress, within twenty-one days after receipt of the latter written declaration, or, if Congress is not in session, within twenty-one days after Congress is required to assemble, determines by two-thirds vote of both Houses that the President is unable

to discharge the powers and duties of his office, the Vice President shall continue to discharge the same as Acting President; otherwise, the President shall resume the powers and duties of his office.

Amendment 26--18-Year-Old-Vote

(Ratified June 30, 1971)

Section 1. The right of citizens of the United States, who are eighteen years of age or older, to vote shall not be denied or abridged by the United States or by any State on account of age.

Section 2. The Congress shall have power to enforce this article by appropriate legislation.

Amendment 27--Compensation- Senators/ Representatives

(Ratified May 7, 1992)

No law, varying the compensation for the services of the Senators and Representatives, shall take effect, until an election of Representatives, shall have intervened.

5

The Declaration of Independence
Action of Second Continental Congress, July 4, 1776
The unanimous Declaration of the thirteen United States of America

When in the Course of human Events, it becomes necessary for one People to dissolve the Political Bands which have connected them with another, and to assume among the Powers of the Earth, the separate and equal Station to which the Laws of Nature and of Nature's God entitle them, a decent Respect to the Opinions of Mankind requires that they should declare the causes which impel them to the Separation.

We hold these truths to be self-evident, that all Men are created equal, that they are endowed by their Creator with certain unalienable Rights, that among these are Life, Liberty, and the Pursuit of Happiness--That to secure these Rights, Governments are instituted among Men, deriving their just Powers from the Consent of the Governed, that whenever any Form of Government becomes destructive of the Ends, it is the Right of the People to alter or to abolish it, and to institute new Government, laying its Foundation on such Principles, and organizing its Powers in such Form, as to them shall seem most likely to effect their Safety and Happiness. Prudence, indeed, will dictate that Governments long established should not be changed for light and transient Causes; and accordingly all Experience hath shewn, that Mankind are more disposed to suffer, while Evils are sufferable, than to right themselves by abolishing the Forms to which they are accustomed. But when a long Train of Abuses and Usurpations, pursuing invariably the same Object, evinces a Design to reduce them under absolute Despotism, it is their Right, it is their Duty, to throw off such Government, and to provide new Guards for their future Security.

Such has been the patient Sufferance of these Colonies; and such is now the Necessity which constrains them to alter their former Systems of Government. The History of repeated Injuries and Usurpations, all having in direct Object the Establishment of an absolute Tyranny over these States. To prove this, let Facts be submitted to a candid World.

HE has refused his Assent to Laws, the most wholesome and necessary for the public Good.

HE has forbidden his Governors to pass Laws of immediate and pressing Importance, unless suspended in their Operation till his Assent should be obtained; and when so suspended, he has utterly neglected to attend to them.

HE has refused to pass other Laws for the Accommodation of large District of People, unless those People would relinquish the Right of Representation in the Legislature, a Right inestimable to them, and formidable to Tyrants only.

HE has called together Legislative Bodies at Places unusual, uncomfortable, and distant from the Depository of their public Records, for the sole Purpose of fatiguing them into Compliance with his Measures.

HE has dissolved Representative Houses repeatedly, for opposing with manly Firmness his Invasions on the Rights of the People.

He has refused for a long Time, after such Dissolutions, to cause others to be elected; whereby the Legislative Powers, incapable of Annihilation, have returned to the People at large for their exercise; the State remaining in the mean time exposed to all the Dangers of Invasion from without, and Convulsions within.

He has endeavoured to prevent the Population of these States; for that Purpose obstructing the Laws for Naturalization of Foreigners; refusing to pass others to encourage their Migrations hither, and raising the Condition of new Appropriations of Lands.

He has obstructed the Administration of Justice, by refusing his Assent to Laws for establishing Judiciary Powers.

He has made Judges dependent on his Will alone, for the Tenure of their Offices, and the Amount and Payment of their Salaries.

HE has erected a Multitude of new Offices, and sent hither Swarms of Officers to harrass our People, and eat out their Substance.

HE has kept among us, in Times of Peace, Standing Armies, without the consent of our Legislatures.

HE has affected to render the Military independent of and superior to the Civil Power.

HE has combined with others to subject us to a Jurisdiction foreign to our Constitution, and unacknowledged by our Laws; giving his Assent to their Acts of pretended Legislation:

FOR quartering large Bodies of Armed Troops among us:

FOR protecting them, by a mock Trial, from Punishment for any Murders which they should commit on the Inhabitants of these States:

FOR cutting off our Trade with all Parts of the World:

FOR imposing Taxes on us without our Consent:

FOR depriving us, in many Cases, of the Benefits of Trial by Jury:

FOR transporting us beyond Seas to be tried for pretended Offences:

FOR abolishing the free System of English Laws in a neighbouring Province, establishing therein an arbitrary Government, and enlarging its Boundaries, so as to render it at once an Example and fit Instrument for introducing the same absolute Rule into these Colonies:

FOR taking away our Charters, abolishing our most valuable Laws, and altering fundamentally the Forms of our Governments:

FOR suspending our own Legislatures, and declaring themselves invested with Power to legislate for us in all Cases whatsoever.

HE has abdicated Government here, by declaring us out of his Protection and waging War against us.

HE has plundered our Seas, ravaged our Coasts, burnt our Towns, and destroyed the Lives of our People.

HE is, at this Time, transporting large Armies of foreign Mercenaries to compleat the Works of Death, Desolation, and Tyranny, already begun with circumstances of Cruelty and Perfidy, scarcely paralleled in the most barbarous Ages, and totally unworthy the Head of a civilized Nation.

HE has constrained our fellow Citizens taken Captive on the high Seas to bear Arms against their Country, to become the Executioners of their Friend and Brethren, or to fall themselves by their Hands.

HE has excited domestic Insurrections amongst us, and has endeavoured to bring on the Inhabitants of our Frontiers, the merciless Indian Savages, whose known Rule of Warfare, is an undistinguished Destruction, of all Ages, Sexes and Conditions.

IN ever   stage of these Oppressions we have Petitioned for Redress in the most humble Terms:

Our repeated Petitions have been answered only by repeated Injury. A Prince, whose Character is thus marked by every act which may define a Tyrant, is unfit to be the Ruler of a free People.

NOR have we been wanting in Attentions to our British Brethren. We have warned them from Time to Time of Attempts by their Legislature to extend an unwarrantable Jurisdiction over us. We have reminded them of the Circumstances of our Emigration and Settlement here, We have appealed to their native Justice and Magnanimity, and we have conjured them by the Ties of our common Kindred to disavow these Usurpations, which, would inevitably interrupt our Connections and Correspondence. They too have been deaf to the Voice of Justice and of Consanguinity. We must, therefore, acquiesce in the Necessity which denounces our Separation, and hold them, as we hold the rest of Mankind, Enemies in War, in Peace, Friends.

WE, therefore, the Representatives of the UNITED STATES OF AMERICA, in GENERAL CONGRESS, Assembled, appealing to the Supreme Judge of the World for the Rectitude of our Intentions, do, in the Name, and by Authority of the good People of these Colonies, solemnly Publish and Declare, That these United Colonies are, and of Right ought to be, FREE AND INDEPENDENT STATES; that they are absolved from all Allegiance to the British Crown, and that all political Connection between them and the State of Great Britain, is and ought to be totally dissolved; and that as FREE AND INDEPENDENT STATES , they have full Power to levy War, conclude Peace, contract Alliances, establish Commerce, and to do all other Acts and things which INDEPENDENT STATES may of right do. And for the support of this Declaration, with a firm Reliance on the Protection of divine Providence, we mutually pledge to each other our Lives, our Fortunes, and our sacred Honor.

Communication Can End Racism

Bridging The Racial Divide Through Interaction With Other Races

Communication

1. Communicate beyond programmed misconceptions

2. Challenge those misconceptions for validity

3. Exchange information by asking questions and answering them

4. Overcoming emotional barriers to communication

One-On-One

(Self-Control and willingness to understand other races
is necessary in this type)

GROUP

(Facilitator or Moderator needed to guide discussions and emotions)

Beginning the Communication Process

1st Step: One-On-One

(If this fails)

2nd Step: Group Participation

(If this fails)

3rd Step: Individual Therapy

(If this fails)

4th Step: Group Therapy

The Onion-Apple Analogy

By
Jeanette Davis

ONION

Peel away the layers of an onion. During the peeling process, each layer peeled away represents the misconceptions we have of other races.

The Purpose is to get to the core of the onion. After peeling to the end, there is no core, thus no substance to our misconceptions.

This proves that stereotypes are only smoke screens that we have of other races. People have to reprogram their minds of all that they have been taught that brands and categorize people of other races, creeds and colors.

APPLE

Peel away the skin of an apple. The removal of the peel is the blinders that have kept us from seeing people as they really are.

Cut the apple in half

The core of the apple is the seed. This represents the essence of each person regardless of race without stereotypical associations.
When planted without discrimination, this seed will grow into a healthy tree with many apples unified and diverse as the branches from which they sprout. This represents America and what it can, and should be.

When communicating with many people of many races, we will eventually find that stereotypes do not exist in reality as in the onion analogy.

There are no smoke screens, but rather real people desiring the same things as you, and that is to pursue life, liberty and the pursuit of happiness.

COMMUNICATION CAN END RACISM

ALL PROBLEMS ARE SOLVABLE

THE RACE PROBLEM IS SOLVABLE

THERE ARE ALWAYS SIMPLE SOLUTIONS TO PROBLEMS. THE KEY IS TO FIND THEM

CONTINUED SEARCHING FOR SOLUTIONS IS THE ANSWER

It is just a matter of how we think about a problem and proceed to solve it. Albert Einstein taught us to view them from many angles to get to the answer.

IT IS A MATTER OF WHO WE THINK PEOPLE ARE AND HOW WE DECIDE TO COMMUNICATE WITH THEM!

WHO ARE AFRICAN-AMERICANS/BLACKS?
All Black People Are Not The Same

Two Diverse Groups

1. Slave Mentality

This group is subservient to dominant culture in varying degrees of passivity. This group will tolerate oppression due to their programming by the dominant group to believe they are inferior. It is difficult for them to change without changes in acceptance of them by the dominant culture. They have varied political points of view, mostly Democratic Party affiliation. Black Republicans are members of this group. Members of this group may join other parties.

2. No Slave Mentality

This group has resisted and, or were never programmed to be subservient due to intervention by family or others during and after slavery, or reprogrammed their minds out of inferiority complexes over time. Also included in this group are Blacks from independent countries outside of the United States. This group also varies by degrees in self worth and high self-esteem to the point of feeling superior to the dominant culture. They have various political points of view, but predominately have Democratic and Independent Party affiliation. Members of this group could participate in other parties.

WHO ARE WHITE AMERICANS?

Many Diverse Groups

- Immigrated from many European countries
- Usually live in clannish neighborhoods of like kind
- Families – Nuclear oriented
- Systematically programmed to feel & think they are superior to other races

Diverse Political Views

- Democratic-Liberal Leanings
- Republican-Conservative
- Independent Party
- Green Party
- Communist Party
- Socialist Party
- Non-Party Affiliation

www.ingramcontent.com/pod-product-compliance
Lightning Source LLC
Chambersburg PA
CBHW060616290526
45793CB00001B/48